MANIFEST DESTINY
AND THE
IMPERIALISM QUESTION

PROBLEMS IN AMERICAN HISTORY

EDITOR

LOREN BARITZ

State University of New York, Albany

MANIFEST DESTINY
AND THE
IMPERIALISM QUESTION

EDITED BY

Charles L. Sanford

Rensselaer Polytechnic Institute

John Wiley & Sons, Inc.

New York · London · Sydney · Toronto

Library of Congress Catologing in Publication Data:

Sanford, Charles L 1920- comp.
Manifest destiny and the imperialism question.

(Problems in American history series)
CONTENTS: Cotton, J. God's promise to New England.
—Box, W. God's providence in Virginia.—Berkeley, G.
On the prospect of planting arts and learning in America. [etc.]
 1. United States—Territorial expansion—Addresses,
essays, lectures. 2. United States—Foreign relations
—Addresses, essays, lectures. I. Title.

E179.5.S24   1974   327.73   74-1398
ISBN 0-471-75320-3
ISBN 0-471-75321-1 (pbk.)

Printed in the United States of America

10 9 8 7 6 5 4 3 2 1

For
Irma Radliff,
who radiates kindness
and good will toward mankind
from her corner grocery store
on Grand Street.

SERIES PREFACE

This series is an introduction to the most important problems in the writing and study of American history. Some of these problems have been the subject of debate and argument for a long time, although others only recently have been recognized as controversial. However, in every case, the student will find a vital topic, an understanding of which will deepen his knowledge of social change in America.

The scholars who introduce and edit the books in this series are teaching historians who have written history in the same general area as their individual books. Many of them are leading scholars in their fields, and all have done important work in the collective search for better historical understanding.

Because of the talent and the specialized knowledge of the individual editors, a rigid editorial format has not been imposed on them. For example, some of the editors believe that primary source material is necessary to their subjects. Some believe that their material should be arranged to show conflicting interpretations. Others have decided to use the selected materials as evidence for their own interpretations. The individual editors have been given the freedom to handle their books in the way that their own experience and knowledge indicate is best. The overall result is a series built up from the individual decisions of working scholars in the various fields, rather than one that conforms to a uniform editorial decision.

A common goal (rather than a shared technique) is the bridge of this series. There is always the desire to bring the reader as close to these problems as possible. One result of this objective is an emphasis of the nature and consequences of problems and events, with a de-emphasis of the more purely historiographical issues. The goal is to involve the student in the reality of crisis, the inevitability of ambiguity, and the excitement of finding a way through the historical maze.

Above all, this series is designed to show students how experienced historians read and reason. Although health is not contagious, intellectual engagement may be. If we show students something significant in a phrase or a passage that they otherwise may have missed, we will have accomplished part of our objective. When students see something that passed us by, then the process will have been made whole. This active and mutual involvement of editor and reader with a significant human problem will rescue the study of history from the smell and feel of dust.

Loren Baritz

ACKNOWLEDGMENTS

I am especially grateful to Michael Dworkin, Howard Green, and my wife Jane Small for calling attention to significant items bearing on Manifest Destiny that I might otherwise have missed. The onus of responsibility I placed on Rensselaer's interlibrary loan staff, particularly Mrs. Rebecca Gould. Her locating and transmitting for my use of rare documents held by other libraries was very great, saving me long hours of expensive telephone calls and travel. Without the cooperation of Rensselaer's Department of Language and Literature in relaxing my teaching and committee duties, publication of this book would have been much delayed. My chief indebtedness, however, is to my immediate family who permitted me the luxury of leisure away from them during the Summer of 1972 for the purpose of completing the manuscript. My foster-daughter Amy Goetz helped my wife in reading copy and in placing Zerox reproductions of original documents on manuscript pages ready for the publisher. The larger family to which I am indebted is the community of fellow scholars who have gone before me, particularly Albert K. Weinberg, Frederick Merk (whose classes I attended at Harvard), and Norman A. Graebner. My emphasis on early and precolonial roots of Manifest Destiny as suggested in this volume by "Quotable Quotes" derives from my study under Perry Miller, Samuel Eliot Morison, and Kenneth Murdock.

TROY, NEW YORK   *Charles L. Sanford*

CONTENTS

MANIFEST DESTINY
AND THE
IMPERIALISM QUESTION

INTRODUCTION

"I used to think," confesses a bitter young man of the 1970s, "that the colonization of the American wilderness was just about the most exciting thing to happen in the history of the whole world." These words launched his review for a college newspaper of Dee Brown's Indian history of the West, *Bury My Heart at Wounded Knee* (New York, ninth printing, 1971). The massacre of 380 Sioux Indians, including women and children, by the United States Cavalry at Wounded Knee, South Dakota, on December 17, 1890 was not only the last bloody event in the securing of the West but has come to symbolize for many Americans the entire history of Indian-white relations.

It also seemingly closed an important chapter in the history of "Manifest Destiny," the great idealizing slogan of American territorial expansion during the nineteenth century. The recent occupation of Wounded Knee by young Indian militants, cheered on by white and black sympathizers, has served notice in large headlines, however, that it is not a closed chapter and, indeed, may need some rewriting. Professional historians, meanwhile, have engaged in a long debate about ways of regarding Manifest Destiny within the total American scheme of things. Informed opinion has covered a wide spectrum, ranging from the view that Manifest Destiny represents a popular aberration with little direct influence on the actual course of history to the view that it expresses a national sense of mission that blazes a trail for better or worse from Plymouth Rock to Vietnam, from a prevailing poverty of material conditions to prosperity, from backward forms of government to enlightened democracy, and from colonial dependency to world power.

Documents in the first section of this book offer an opportunity to explore the historic origins of Manifest Destiny, which historians generally date from about 1830. John L. O'Sullivan's 1845 article that coined the precise phrasing, "Manifest Destiny," appears in this section, but other documents suggest that its underlying premises were operative during the early colonial period. These premises were articulated with ardent conviction from New England to Georgia—namely, that the colonists were a chosen people divinely appointed to occupy the largely vacant lands of the New World, that they had a special mission from God to spread the "new light" of the Gospel throughout the wilderness and ultimately throughout the world, that savages and other enemies who resisted conversion could be righteously exterminated as creatures of Satan, and that this mission manifested itself in the unfolding of providential history since the Protestant Reformation and discovery of America, which followed the course of the Sun from east to west. This is the main import of what John Cotton, William Box, Bishop Berkeley, and Nathaniel Ames have to tell us from out of the colonial past.

Their testimonies make for some difficult but rewarding reading that clarifies much that follows. The major difficulty is one of language which, although grammatical enough for parsing, is studded with archaic usages, Biblical allusions, and strange logic. The strangeness derives from a form of theological suasion designed to make facts square with divine revelation. If the reader will keep in mind the view that Manifest Destiny was a secular religion stemming from such thought, he should have little difficulty with this section. Also he should be aware that it contains all the inherent contradictions that have bothered professional historians ever since. One is the sordid taint of profit—sordid only by comparison with grand professions of benevolence blessed by God. And yet this blend of practicality and idealism is not far removed from the industrial executive who stated that the interest of General Motors is the interest of the United Sates. One is also reminded of Adam Smith's "invisible hand," a ghostly guarantee that the unencumbered pursuit of private self-interest would benefit everybody. It remains a major premise of capitalism. When this ideal fell short of practice, the stewards of great wealth created philanthropic foundations. Not content with Adam Smith's euphemism, John D. Rockefeller claimed that his own stewardship came directly from God.

Many Americans, including the notable scions of great wealth like Nelson Rockefeller, Franklin D. Roosevelt, Averell Harriman, and John F. Kennedy, have not agreed that philanthropy can take up the slack between self-interest and the public welfare. If it could—so the argument goes—chronic poverty would be largely eliminated, mineral resources would not have been so recklessly exploited, the natural environment would be more wholesome, the inner cities would not be deteriorating, and perhaps racial minorities would have achieved a place in the American sun commensurate with their native abilities. The latter consideration constitutes a very big "perhaps," because American racism, a special case of failure within the democratic dogma of equal opportunity, has deep roots in Western history. Although historians have been disturbed by the racism in Manifest Destiny rhetoric, few have paid attention to a seemingly poetic device by which it was justified, a device fairly common to colonial literature.

This was homage to the sun in its transit from east to west, which originally figured in the religious millennial context mentioned above, not as poetry but as prophetic fact. This sun symbolism needs analysis because it helped to mediate a shift in popular sentiment from God to man and nature. It expressed feelings so deeply imbedded as to short-circuit the kind of rational discourse for which Benjamin Franklin is famous. In fact, Franklin has been omitted from this collection in favor of his nearest almanac rival, Nathaniel Ames, who better represents the continuity between colonial feeling and Manifest Destiny's high noon. Franklin prefigured the westward movement in calculated Malthusian terms; Ames prefigured it in sun-blown rhetoric. Briefly, sun symbolism suggested the will of God, the reign of nature, the course of history, undiluted happiness and prosperity, and most especially the future destiny of a chosen people who possessed fair skins and blue eyes like the sky. The recent popular designation for this psychological complex is WASP—otherwise known as white Anglo-Saxon Protestants, a complex shared by many Americans of different ethnic origin and religious faith.

Berkeley's poem, "Westward the Course of Empire," derives its central meaning from sun symbolism, a meaning hardly confined to geography (of which more later). In this reading, the sun supposedly shines on a favored people who distinguish themselves by deeds; other peoples remain in darkness until "saved" by their superiors. This messianic impulse within Manifest Destiny has also troubled professional historians. Thus, in colonial documents, American Indians are considered as inferiors who must give way to a superior race. Blacks are seldom mentioned. After 1854, the year which opened the "Kansas Question," Negro slaves began to displace Indians from the centers of messianic interest. The Northern carrier of Manifest Destiny in this new context was John Brown at Pottowatomie; his Southern counterpart was William Walker—both instruments of colonial premises that erupted into the Civil War, a major cause of which had to do with conflicting notions of national mission in the settlement of new western territories.

The colonial period encompassed roughly 170 years, a period almost equal in time to the national experience and, therefore, formative of whatever national character the United States can be said to possess, a major ingredient of which has been to crusade for causes at home and abroad. At home, the unifying cause that Manifest Destiny represented began to split over the economic issue of free and slave labor in the territories. Once this was resolved, it acquired a new life abroad and brought new internal divisions. At no time, however, were colonial Bibles left far behind. Thus, read for the five or seven apocalyptic stages of biblical prophecy converging on the American continent, Charles Darwin's grand evolutionary scheme, with Americans at the apex. For the Old Testament's "saving remnant," read "survival of the fittest." For the influx of immigrants from Southeastern Europe since 1890 who threatened by weight of numbers and skills the old Anglo-Saxon dominance, substitute the concept of "English-speaking Peoples"—and you have colonial scripture fairly intact.

In this outcome, colonial sun symbolism was predictive in the sense that it helped to bring about its own validation. As Ralph Waldo Emerson said, "Nothing important is done without enthusiasm." Enthusiasm is a product of faith, a product greatly in demand by any people unsure of itself, as Americans have been since colonial days—a people frequently scorned by British progenitors as "rabble" and constantly augmented by emigrants from other lands and races. For a time, then, Manifest Destiny reigned as the common denominator of all differences, a secular national religion to whose flag all but the so-called "colored races" could rally. Sun symbolism not only reinforced racist attitudes and millennial expectations; it suggested and led the westward trek of civilization. This last point has to be made with considerable force, because professional historians like Professor Norman Graebner have argued that advocates of Manifest Destiny lacked a sense of direction (both as to ends and means). Other historians have noted designs on Canada, Cuba, Mexico, and South America, frequently interpreting the acquisition of Alaska as an example of pretensions to the whole of North and South America. Quite to the contrary, the one thing about which preachers of Manifest Destiny were most sure was that the future lay westward, following the sun, and *not* north or south.

Of course, there were adventurers, several of them represented here, who dreamed of American hegemony over both continents. Hardly an adventurer, Secretary of State Seward under President Lincoln, for instance, envisaged a capital city at Mexico which would govern North and South America. The significant aspect about such speculation is that on its idealistic side, as opposed to the purely commercial, the announced intention was almost always to consolidate the Americas in the westward thrust of civilization prior to redeeming the Orient for Christian democracy. Thus both Alaska and the Panama Canal were sold to the American people as investments in the fabulous passage to India. This outcome could have been predicted on the basis of intelligence from the colonial period. Colonial experience also prepared popular opinion for a self-abnegating world responsibility. It was stated quite baldly in Bishop Berkeley's famous line, "Westward the course of empire takes its way," which contained a sense of destiny widely held even among colonists who did not dream of separation from the mother country.

Thus, although the westward movement, in and of itself, lacked a conscious ideal of a continent-wide destiny and though national political leaders constantly read the great god Terminus in a succession of seemingly natural barriers to further expansion, beginning with the Allegheny Mountains, a dynamic design operated to favor the occupation of contiguous territories to the

west over lands to the north and south. Historians who argue
that the westward movement can be explained by the economics
of land hunger in response to a largely empty continent inviting
to be filled, fail adequately to take into account the power of an
idea. Before leaving the colonial documents, we should examine
this idea more thoroughly in its formative period, particularly its
messianic character, which has put a great strain on Americans
collectively ever since, not only to demonstrate the superiority of
their institutions but to have them adopted by other peoples.
This consideration leads to a question most hotly debated by historians: whether Manifest Destiny should be understood as the
ideology of American imperialism? A related question is whether
Manifest Destiny applies to extracontinental territorial ambition.

We have already pointed out that it did not include any notion
of our present continental boundaries, only a vision of a superi-
or, westward-expanding civilization. Superior to what? While the
colonial documents in this collection do not address this question
directly, they certainly suggest a determination to advance the
Protestant faith and to avoid the supposed mistakes of European
society. One gathers that the major enemy through whom Satan
worked was the European powers who were then contending for
supremacy on the American continent. Hence, there was from
the beginning an almost paranoid thrust away from Europe. On
its negative side, a fear and distrust of things European became a
major theme of Manifest Destiny that contributed to its westward course. Significantly, when American interest leaped overseas, it was still propelled westward toward the Far East, gob-
bling up Hawaii along the way. There was no inherent reason
not to expand north and south instead, since the inhabitants of
those areas, except for British Canada, were—as many American journalists said—like ripe fruit ready to be plucked. Latin
American states won their independence with scarcely a major
battle. The United States government reacted to temptation with
the Monroe Doctrine which, in its original form, simply warned
European powers not to encroach further on the Western Hemisphere.

Now we come to the heart of the imperialist issue. The authoritative view is that of Harvard historian, Frederick Merk:
"Imperialism was the antithesis of Manifest Destiny." This view

holds that the Monroe Doctrine was largely defensive, that Manifest Destiny, in and of itself, held no extraterritorial ambitions, and that it was an adjunct to the westward movement of population that expressed faith in the spread of democratic institutions. In oher words, Merk would separate Manifest Destiny from the jingoistic nationalism that accompanied the American flag into the Philippines in 1898 and presumably, if he were alive, would deny its relevance to American involvement overseas since 1898. Merk arrived at this conclusion first from preconceptions favoring the frontier as a democratizing influence, following in the wake of his famous mentor, Frederick Jackson Turner; and second by restricting his study to the interplay between influential journalism and recorded event. Within these limits, we have no reason to doubt that Manifest Destiny sentiment flourished along frontier outposts, with greatest encouragementa from Jacksonian Democrats, abetted by Puritan descendants like John Quincy Adams and Charles Summer. New England, as a whole, for reasons of industrialism remained lukewarm, while both New England and the South quickly divided over the issue of color.

The clearest demarcation between phases one and two of Manifest Destiny comes from an older historian who bears quoting because he represents a kind of poet laureate on the subject with which most professional historians can relate even today. In a public address at Yale University, Professor Ephraim D. Adams concluded in 1913 that there were two phases of Manifest Destiny:

". . . the earlier expressing merely the conviction of superiority in our form of government and the greater happiness of our people; while the later phase carried with this belief the desire for new territory, and the responsibility of imposing upon other nations the benefits of our own. Present-day judgment repudiates the latter view, while holding firmly to the faith in our institutions, and to confidence in our future. In that ideal of manifest destiny,—a belief in our institutions, as the best in the world adapted to secure to *our* people 'life, liberty, and the pursuit of happiness,'—we may still assert our faith."

This view summarizes the defense, the gist of which is ultimately moral. Critics like Denna F. Fleming, however, arrive at oppo-

site conclusions: that "Manifest Destiny" is just another name
for American imperialism, and such critics will not separate
phase one from phase two.

Imperialism is commonly defined as control over foreign peoples against their will. Once colonial subjects of England, their
very survival threatened by rival European powers, Americans
have traditionally opposed imperialism both for themselves and
for other nations, as a wicked European game. Yet John Adams
predicted in 1787 that the 13 new American republics were
"destined to spread over the northern part of that whole quarter
of the globe . . . in favor of the rights of mankind." His son,
John Quincy Adams, in formulating the Monroe Doctrine, told
the British ministry straight away that everyone must consider all
of North America to be controlled by the United States. An out-
spoken critic of European imperialism, President Jefferson was
responsible for the largest acquisition of territory in American
history, the Louisiana Purchase. A popular biographer of the
late nineteenth century hailed the "destined moment . . . when
Anglo-Saxon supremacy over the New West . . . will give law to
the rest of the world." John Hay, Secretary of State under Theodore Roosevelt, supported an open door policy in China to give
American interests there an equal footing with European powers.
President Woodrow Wilson sent expeditionary forces to Europe
to "make the world safe for democracy." Such statements and
deeds represent the paradox of Manifest Destiny,—indeed, of
the American people.

The single most consistent theme of the foregoing documents,
beginning with the colonial testimonies, is messianic. This is as
true of critics as of advocates of Manifest Destiny, and it may
provide the key for resolving the paradox of innocence and guilt
in an expanding American influence that numerous Europeans,
since William Stead in 1901, have called "The Americanization
of the World." What is usually implied in the latter phrase by
Europeans is not at all a classical pattern of imperialism—political domination of foreign peoples by means of military forces—
but, instead, a cultural infiltration typified by our American
music, movies, slang, and very especially by technology and mana-
gerial know-how. Only very recently, almost since the Watergate
revelations, has the question of political manipulation by Ameri-

cans of foreign governments been raised. There have been exceptions of overt political intervention in the so-called "bananna republics" of Central and South America, also of flagrant espionage such as the much publicized U-2 incident over Russia and the *Pueblo* sneakery in Korean waters. These latter incidents have been justified in the interest of national security. American intervention in Central and South America cannot be so easily passed off, and yet it is not imperialism in the European pattern of colonial domination. The major United States example of European imperialism has been the Philippines, which was finally granted independence in 1916. All other American acquisitions have been either by annexation, as with Hawaii, by purchase as with Louisiana and Alaska, or by cession as with Guam and Puerto Rico. The European pattern of military conquest and political domination does not seem to hold for the United States.

Then why the continuing charge of American imperialism by critics of Manifest Destiny? A possible answer to this question, which is argued through every document in this book, may lie in the conflicting views of national mission that had something to do with the adjustment of means to ends. Thus, while Americans generally expected to exert a favorable influence over the rest of mankind, they often disagreed on the means employed. Their messianic heritage encompassed two rather different courses: one being the path of activistic proseletyzing that led by degrees to various forms of coercion, not excluding the use of military force; and the other relying on the quiet force of exemplary conduct. The strictures of Presidents Washington and Jefferson against entangling alliances belong to the *messianic example*— more popularly known as "isolationism." President Theodore Roosevelt's invocation of a police power over Latin America as a corollary to the Monroe Doctrine converted that doctrine into an expression of *messianic intervention*—sometimes confused with enlightened internationalism. As is suggested by Jefferson's purchase of Louisiana contrary to his constitutional scruples, a clear line cannot be drawn between these two concepts of national mission. Although Manifest Destiny represents the vocal high tide of messianic intervention, its chief proponents made the same claim to national virtue as did their detractors.

Indeed, the aura of virture with which Manifest Destiny surrounded territorial greed largely accounted for its popular sway. Its psychological function was precisely to discharge Americans of the kind of guilt associated with colonial domination and imperialism, and its ideology was in some ways consistent with constitutional restraints against naked imperialism. We now consider what credence it gave to charges of imperialism during its continental phase, which began about 1830 and closed with the Civil War. Within the context of imperialism, the Louisiana Purchase of 1803 initially presented little difficulty, because the aggrieved parties were not France and Spain, but American Indians who did not know that they were aggrieved until many years later. Differences with Mexico then led to the acquisitions of Texas, New Mexico, and California, to which Manifest Destiny gave both sanction and encouragement. Were these instances of imperialism?

Certainly, John L. O'Sullivan, as is revealed below, did not think so, even though he expected that the United States would have to go to war to preserve these territories; and he blamed Mexico for the resulting war. In the document included here, he directs his reasoning expressly to the issue of imperialism. He reasons that destiny itself "manifestly" favored American hegemony over these territories because of superior institutions and people, because of the remoteness of a weak Mexican government, because American settlers were already infiltrating the area in large numbers and would ask to be incorporated into the Union in the manner prescribed by the Constitution, and—not least—because destiny had made science a timely instrument for cementing the New West to the United States by means of telegraph and railroad. In essence, his widely influential argument joined the long-existing messianic impulse to a new scientific spirit wherein the role of God was largely replaced by natural law—or "Destiny"—and the weight of divine revelation was replaced by supposedly scientific and historical proof—or that which was "manifest." Thomas Hart Benton, in another document included here, made much the same argument for the acquisition of Oregon. During phase two of Manifest Destiny, which dates roughly from 1898 to the present and has to do with extraterritorial ambition in the section entitled "The Civilization Trust," the only major ideological contribution to Manifest Destiny was to translate the colonial calendar of millennial stages of history into the evolutionary ideas of Charles Darwin and to update the nineteenth-century idea of progress along scientific lines. The champions of Manifest Destiny read history as a linear process culminating in a more or less permanent American world hegemony of virtue. Its (rather few) detractors tended toward a cyclical view of history in which nations and civilizations rise and fall through their own internal defects.

In deciding whether Manifest Destiny was an ideology of imperialism akin to that of, say, Britain's "The White Man's Burden," Tolstoi's concept of "Mother Russia," the French *mission civilisatrice,* or Japan's more recent dreams of a "Greater Co-Prosperity Sphere" for Asia, one must make certain observations. The first one is the self-abnegating character of Manifest Destiny, which proclaims in essence that Americans are more agents than actors in a world drama whose outcome has depended not on ordinary men and women but on God or natural law since the foundation of the universe. The second observation is that Americans rely on supposed scientific proofs for their beliefs more than any other people except the Russians. A third observation is that Americans have made a fetish of their Constitution, which gives specific rules for assimilating new territory to governmental jurisdiction. A fourth observation, which is necessarily ironic, opening a wide door to critics of American imperialism, is that Rudyard Kipling's poem, "The White Man's Burden," was first published in the United States with America's role after the Spanish-American War in mind.

Kipling's famous poem is commonly understood by Americans as an expression of hateful British imperialism. A native American equivalent published in 1871—not reprinted here because it is both lengthy and well-known—would be Walt Whitman's poem, "Passage to India," which envisages the movement of civilization from its birth to a fulfillment in the West, reaching across the Pacific Ocean, finally, to forge a last link with ancient Asiatic origins. This mystical vision of encircling the globe from East to West with a superior civilization under American auspices comprehends the fullest meaning of Manifest Destiny in both its continental and extracontinental phases. Whiteman's statement differs significantly from Kipling's in its warm democratic sympathies, defining the United States as the nation of nations destined for world leadership primarily because it was an amalgam of all peoples and races. Perhaps it is true that any fundamental, thoroughgoing democracy must be at odds with the kind of subjection of peoples that has characterized the old imperialism. Yet the United States constituted in practice an imperfect amalgam whose westward spread of settlements required the subjugation of certain peoples against their will. Even if we leave aside the question of black slavery, one could argue that the continental period of American expansion was, at least, as imperialistic as the later period. A section of this volume, therefore, considers the pros and cons of the American Indian question.

The last two sections deal with extracontinental expansion, beginning with the acquisition of Alaska. These confront us with several related problems. The first, and most important, is whether the basic premises of Manifest Destiny, established during the colonial experience, undergo any radical shift between the time of continental expansion and that of extracontinental involvement (continentalism meaning the present east-west boundaries of the United States less the states of Alaska and Hawaii) . A second related problem is whether the second phase of Manifest Destiny, which usually dates from 1898, can be considered more imperialistic that the first. A third is whether the phrase "Manifest Destiny" does not perhaps imply a new form of imperialism quite unlike the example of imperial Rome which other major Western nations have followed. A final, crucial question is whether Manifest Destiny really applies, as the last document suggests, to American involvement in Vietnam.

The issue of imperialism is not at all settled. Highly respected historical authority argues that Manifest Destiny belongs to continentalism, the antithesis of imperialism. A friendly British historian, Denis Brogan, calls us "the new imperial power" in the sense that we "expect the world to turn American," with a corresponding duty to "police the world." On the other hand, a recent book-length study of President Nixon's foreign policy applauds him for a strategic retreat from world power commensurate with traditional democratic practice. In the final analysis, the reader must make up his own mind about the arguments and evidence that are presented here.

PART ONE

Roots of Manifest Destiny

QUOTABLE QUOTES

"They thinke that the contemplacion of nature, and the prayse thereof cumminge, is to God a very acceptable honour."

Sir Thomas More, 1516

"God would show him the new land as he did to Moses and Aaron after so long a struggle. For that was God's promise."

Lope de Vega, 1614

"O brave new world!"

Shakespeare, ca. 1610

"And that which still aggrevates their Crimes the more, and must needs farther provoke the Divine Displeasure, is, that God had made choice of *Spain* to carry his blessed Gospel into the *Indies,* and to bring many populous Nations to the knowledge of himself."

Bartholomew de las Casas, 1544

". . . it has always been our principal Intention to cause the Light of the Gospel to shine on the People of the New World."

Queen Isabella, ca. 1494

"It seemes, this end in plantation, hath been especially reserved for this later end of the world by reason of the progress of the light of the Gospel from East to West in this last age."

John White, 1630

13

"And seeing Lord the highest end of our plantation here, is to set up the standard, & display the banner of Jesus Christ, even here where Satans throne is Lord, let our labor be blessed in laboring the conversion of the heathen."

William Strachey, 1612

1 FROM

John Cotton
God's Promise to New England

In this address, Reverend John Cotton bid farewell to John Winthrop's company, departing Southampton, England in 1630 to find the Massachusetts Bay colony. Although Cotton did not invent the ideas enunciated here out of whole cloth, he neverthe-less gave a concise formulation to the ideology that governed the Puritan "Errand into the Wilderness." His statement is important not only because it contains the seeds of Manifest Destiny but because it represents the collective voice of a people who became the chief carriers of Manifest Destiny across the continent. Cot-ton later became an influential spiritual leader in Massachusetts. His Biblical language here, based on a text from 2 Sam. 7:10, hardly conceals a chosen people's grand design to dispossess the Indians from their lands by fair means or foul.

Now God makes room for a people 3 wayes:

First, when he casts out the enemies of a people before them by lawfull warre with the inhabitants, which God cals them unto: as in *Ps.* 44. 2. *Thou didst drive out the heathen before them.*

SOURCE. John Cotton, *God's Promise to His Plantations* (London, 1630), reprinted as *Old South Leaflet,* No. 53, pp. 5–8.

But this course of warring against others, & driving them out without provocation, depends upon speciall Commission from God, or else it is not imitable.

Secondly, when he gives a forreigne people favour in the eyes of any native people to come and sit downe with them either by way of purchase, as *Abraham* did obtaine the field of *Machpelah;* or else when they give it in courtesie, as *Pharaoh* did the land of *Goshen* unto the sons of *Jacob.*

Thirdly, when hee makes a Countrey though not altogether void of inhabitants, yet voyd in that place where they reside. Where there is a vacant place, there is liberty for the sonne of *Adam* or *Noah* to come and inhabite, though they neither buy it, nor aske their leaves. *Abraham* and *Isaac,* when they sojourned amongst the Philistines, they did not buy that land to feede their cattle, because they said There is roome enough. And so did *Jacob* pitch his Tent by *Sechem, Gen.* 34. 21. There was *roome enough* as *Hamor* said, *Let them sit down amongst us.* And in this case if the people who were former inhabitants did disturbe them in their possessions, they complained to the King, as of wrong done unto them: As *Abraham* did because they took away his well, in *Gen.* 21. 25. For his right whereto he pleaded not his immediate calling from God, (for that would have seemed frivolous amongst the Heathen) but his owne industry and culture in digging the well, verse 30. Nor doth the King reject his plea, with what had he to doe to digge wells in their soyle? but admitteth it as a Principle in Nature, That in a vacant soyle, hee that taketh possession of it, and bestoweth culture and husbandry upon it, his Right it is. And the ground of this is from the grand Charter given to *Adam* and his posterity in Paradise, *Gen.* 1. 28. *Multiply, and replenish the earth, and subdue it.* If therefore any sonne of *Adam* come and finde a place empty, he hath liberty to come, and fill, and subdue the earth there. This Charter was renewed to *Noah, Gen.* 9. 1. *Fulfill the earth and multiply:* So that it is free from that comon Grant for any to take possession of vacant Countries. Indeed no Nation is to drive out another without speciall Commission from heaven, such as the Israelites had, unless the Natives do unjustly wrong them, and will not recompence the wrongs done in peaceable sort, & then they may right themselves by lawfull war, and subdue the Countrey unto themselves.

This placeing of people in this or that Countrey, is from Gods soveraignty over all the earth, and the inhabitants thereof: as in *Psal.* 24. 1. *The earth is the Lords, and the fulnesse thereof.* And in *Ier.* 10. 7. God is there called, *The King of Nations:* and in *Deut.* 10. 14. Therefore it is meete he should provide a place for all Nations to inhabite, and haue all the earth replenished. Onely in the Text here is meant some more speciall appointment, because God tells them it by his owne mouth; he doth not so with other people, he doth not tell the children of *Sier,* that hee hath appointed a place for them: that is, He gives them the land by promise; others take the land by his providence, but Gods people take the land by promise: And therefore the land of *Canaan* is called a land of promise. Which they discerne, first, by discerning themselves to be in Christ, in whom all the promises are yea, and amen.

Secondly, by finding his holy presence with them, to wit, when he plants them in the holy Mountaine of his Inheritance: *Exodus.* 15. 17. And that is when he giveth them the liberty and purity of his Ordinances. It is a land of promise, where they have provision for soule as well as for body. *Ruth* dwelt well for outward respects while shee dwelt in *Moab,* but when shee cometh to dwell in *Israel,* shee is said to come under the wings of God: *Ruth* 2. 12. When God wrappes us in with his Ordinances, and warmes us with the life and power of them as with wings, there is a land of promise.

This my teach us all where we doe now dwell, or where after wee may dwell, be sure you looke at every place appointed to you, from the hand of God: wee may not rush into any place, and never say to God, By your leave; but we must discerne how God appoints us this place. There is poore comfort in sitting down in any place, that you cannot say, This place is appointed me of God. Canst thou say that God spied out this place for thee, and there hath setled thee above all hindrances? didst thou finde that God made roome for thee either by lawfull descent, or purchase, or gift, or other warrantable right? Why then this is the place God hath appointed thee; here hee hath made roome for thee, he hath placed thee in *Rehoboth,* in a peaceable place: This we must discerne, or els we are but intruders upon God. And when wee doe withall discerne, that God giveth us these outward blessings from his love in Christ, and maketh comfortable provision as well for our soule as for our bodies, by the meanes of grace, then doe we enjoy our present possession as well by gracious promise, as by the common, and just, and bountifull providence of the Lord. Or if a man doe remove, he must see that God hath espied out such a Countrey for him.

2   FROM   *William Box*
God's Providence in Virginia

An enduring myth of American history has it that the Southern colonists were an irreligious lot of fortune seekers compared to the New England saints. William Box's narrative of early Virginia may suggest otherwise. Actually, these colonists were also children of the Protestant Reformation who tended to see the hand of God in their worldly undertakings and were quite as quick to take up arms against imagined minions of the devil. If the visible church figured less prominently in their governance, an important reason was the relatively relaxed sway of Anglicanism. Yet the Virginian assembly early passed strict "blue laws." Reverend Daniel Price's farewell sermon for the Virginia Adventurers in 1609 differed from its New England counterpart chiefly in descrying a land already overflowing with milk and honey. When the colony did not prosper in this "garden of the world," its members were accused of sloth and worldly vanity. Box's narrative deals with the "time of starvation," ended by the late arrival of Lord Delaware—who promptly succumbed to the same combination of malaria, dysentery, and scurvy that had afflicted the settlers in the mosquito-infested swampland that was early Jamestown.

SOURCE. John Smith's *Generall Historie.* . . (London, 1624) as reprinted in *Narratives of Early Viginia, 1606–1625,* edited by Lyon Gardiner Tyler (New York: Charles Scribner's Sons, 1907) , pp. 297–301.

His Lordship arrived the ninth of June 1610. accompanied with Sir Ferdinando Waynman, Captaine Houlcroft, Captaine Lawson, and divers other Gentlemen of sort; the tenth he came up with his fleet, went on shore, heard a Sermon, read his Commission, and entred into consultation for the good of the Colonie: in which secret counsell we will a little leave them, that we may duly observe the revealed counsell of God. Hee that shall but turne up his eie, and behold the spangled canopie of heaven, or shall but cast downe his eie, and consider the embroydered carpet of the earth, and withall shall marke how the heavens heare the earth, and the earth the Corne and Oile, and they relieve the necessities of man, that man will acknowledge Gods infinite providence. But hee that shall further observe, how God inclineth all casuall events to worke the necessary helpe of his Saints, must needs adore the Lord infinite goodnesse. Never had any people more just cause, to cast themselves at the very footstoole of God, and to reverence his mercies, than this distressed Colonie; for if God had not sent Sir Thomas Gates from the Bermudas, within foure daies they had almost beene famished; if God had not directed the heart of that noble Knight to save the Fort from fiering at their shipping, for many were very importunate to have burnt it, they had beene destitute of a present harbour and succour: if they had abandoned the Fort any longer time, and had not so soone returned, questionlesse the Indians would have destroied the Fort, which had beene the meanes of our safeties amongst them and a terror. If they had set saile sooner, and had lanched into the vast Ocean; who would have promised they should have incountered the Fleet of the Lord la Ware: especially when they made for Newfound land, as they intended; a course contrarie to our Navie approaching. If the Lord la Ware had not brought with him a yeeres provision, what comfort would those poore soules have received, to have beene relanded to a second distruction? This was the arme of the Lord of Hosts, who would have his people passe the red Sea and Wildernesse, and then to possesse the land of Canaan: It was divinely spoken of Heathen Socrates, If God for man be carefull, why should man bee over-distrustfull? for he hath so tempered the contrary qualities of the Elements,

That neither cold things want heat, nor moist things dry,
Nor sad things spirits, to quicken them thereby,
Yet make they music all content of contrarietie,
Which conquer'd, knits them in such links together,
They doe produce even all this whatsoever.

The Lord Governour, after mature deliberation, delivered some few words to the Companie, laying just blame upon them, for their haughtie vanities and sluggish idlenesse, earnestly intreating them to amend those desperate follies lest hee should be compelled to draw the sword of Justice and to cut off such delinquents, which he had rather draw to the shedding of his vitall bloud, to protect them from injuries; heartning them with relation of that store hee had brought with him, constituting officers of all conditions, to rule over them, allotting every man his particular place, to watch vigilantly, and worke painfully. This Oration and direction being received with a generall applause, you might shortly behold the idle and restie diseases of a divided multitude, by the unitie and authorities of this government to be substantially cured. Those that knew not the way to goodnesse before, but cherished singularitie and faction, can now chalke out the path of all respective dutie and service: every man endevoureth to outstrip other in diligence: the French preparing to plant the Vines, the English labouring in the Woods and grounds; every man knoweth his charge, and dischargeth the same with alacritie. Neither let any man be discouraged, by the relation of their daily labour (as though the sap of their bodies should bee spent for other mens profit) the setled times of working, to effect all themselves, or as the Adventurers need desire, required no more paines than from six of the clocke in the morning, untill ten, and from two in the afternoone, till foure; at both which times they are provided a spirituall and corporall reliefe. First, they enter into the Church, and make their praiers unto God; next they returne to their houses and receive their proportion of food. Nor should it bee conceived that this businesse excludeth Gentlemen, whose breeding never knew what a daies labour meant: for though they cannot digge, use the Spade, nor practice the Axe, yet may the staied spirits of any condition, finde how to imploy the force of knowledge, the exercise of

counsell, the operation and power of thier best breeding and qualities. The houses which are built, are as warme and defensive
against wind and weather, as if they were tiled and slated, being
covered above with strong boards, and some matted round with
Indian mats. Our forces are now such as are able to tame the fu-
rie and trecherie of the Salvages: Our Forts assure the Inhabitants, and frustrate all assaylants. . . .

The fertilitie of the soile, the temperature of the climate, the
forme of government, the condition of our people, their daily in-
vocating of the Name of God being thus expressed; why should
the successe, by the rules of mortall judgement, bee disparaged?
why should not the rich harvest of our hopes be seasonably expected? I dare say, that the resolution of Cæsar in France, the
designes of Alexander, the discoveries of Hernando Cortes in the
West, and of Emanuel King of Portugal in the East, were not encouraged upon so firme grounds of state and possibilitie.

3   FROM   *George Berkeley*
*On the Prospect of Planting Arts and Learning
in America*

*George Berkeley (1685–1753), the famous philosopher and
Anglican bishop, wrote this poem in 1726, shortly before setting
sail for America, where he hoped to establish a college for the
conversion of Indians. Failing in this mission for want of funds,
he returned to England several years later, a disappointment
which suggests that this more humane method of dealing with Indians did not always receive the highest priority in the colonies.
In any event, missionary activity of this kind has come to be suspect as another face of imperialism.*

*The poem is notable for several reasons. First, it marks the
transition from religious to a more secular idealism. Second, it
strikes the distinctly prophetic note that was to characterize*

SOURCE. *The Works of George Berkeley* (Oxford: the Clarendon Press,
1901) , IV, pp. 365–366.

Manifest Destiny. Third, it announces in a few memorable phrases the great American theme of nature and civilization. Its great and continuing popularity with American readers dates from 1752, when it was first published in the British magazine, Miscellany.

The Muse, disgusted at an age and clime
    Barren of every glorious theme,
In distant lands now waits a better time,
    Producing subjects worthy fame:

In happy climes, where from the genial sun
    And virgin earth such scenes ensue,
The force of art by nature seems outdone,
    And fancied beauties by the true:

In happy climes, the seat of innocence,
    Where nature guides and virtue rules,
Where men shall not impose for truth and sense
    The pedantry of courts and schools:

There shall be sung another golden age,
    The rise of empire and of arts,
The good and great inspiring epic rage,
    The wisest heads and noblest hearts.

Not such as Europe breeds in her decay;
    Such as she bred when fresh and young,
When heavenly flame did animate her clay,
    By future poets shall be sung.

Westward the course of empire takes its way;
    The four first acts already past,
A fifth shall close the drama with the day;
    Time's noblest offspring is the last.

4 FROM *Nathaniel Ames*
America—Its Past, Present, and Future State

Almanac-maker, jester, and prophet of destiny as of the weather eight years before Benjamin Franklin launched his "Poor Richard's Almanac," Ames in this essay gives Berkeley's famous line, "Westward the course of empire takes its way," the kind of specificity and lively relevance that it has since acquired for itself through historic fulfillment. With Ames, whose almanacs are reputed to have reached a larger audience throughout New England than did any other single form of expression at the time, the dynamic east-west thrust of American society has been well established, and its classic enemy has been well defined as devilish European powers. With Ames, too, the mission of regeneration has largely shifted from Christian crusade to civilizing saviordom. A major unresolved problem that Ames cautiously skirts is how to restore an imagined golden age in its innocent pastoral setting and also create great cities. Ames has obviously read Berkeley's poem.

America is a Subject which daily becomes more and more interesting:—I shall therefore fill these Pages with a Word upon its Past, Present and Future State.

I. First of its Past State: Time has cast a Shade upon this Scene.—Since the Creation innumerable Accidents have happened here, the bare mention of which would create Wonder and Surprize; but they are all lost in Oblivion: The ignorant Natives for Want of Letters have forgot their Stock; and know not from whence they came, or how, or when they arrived here, or what has happened since:—Who can tell what wonderful Changes

SOURCE. Nathaniel Ames, "America—Its Past, Present, and Future State," *Astronomical Diary and Almanac* (Boston, 1758), n. p. This essay concludes the almanac and is not formally titled.

have happen'd by the mighty Operations of Nature, such as De-
luges, Vulcanoes, Earthquakes, etc.!—Or whether great Tracts
of Land were not absorbed into those vast Lakes or inland Seas
which occupy so much Space to the West of us.—But to leave the
Natural, and come to the Political State: We know how the
French have erected a Line of Forts from the *Ohio* to *Nova-Sco-
tia,* including all the inestimable Country to the West of us, into
their exorbitant Claim.—This, with infinite Justice, the *English*
resented; & in this Cause our Blood has been spilled: Which
brings to our Consideration,

II. Secondly, The Present State of North America.—A Writer
upon this present Time says, "The Parts of *North America*
which may be claimed by *Great Britain* or *France* are of as
much Worth as either Kingdom.—That fertile Country to the
West of the Appalachian Mountains (a String of 8 or 900 miles
in length) between *Canada* and the *Mississippi,* is of larger extent than all *France, Germany* and *Poland;* and all well provided
with rivers, a very fine wholesome air a rich Soil, capable of pro-
ducing Food and Physick, and all Things necessary for the Con-
veniency and Delight of Life: In fine, the Garden of the World!"
—Time was we might have been possessed of it: At this Time
two mighty Kings contend for this inestimable Prize:—Their respective Claims are to be measured by the Length of their
Swords.—The Poet says, The Gods and Opportunity ride Post;
that you must take her by the Forelock being bald Behind.—
Have we not too fondly depended upon our Numbers?—Sir
Francis Bacon says, 'The Wolf careth not how many the Sheep
be:' But Numbers well—spirited, with the Blessing of Heaven
will do Wonders, when by miliary Skill and Discipline, the Com-
manders can actuate (as by one Soul) the most numerous Bodies of arm'd People:—Our numbers will not avail till the Colonies are united; for whilst divided, the Strength of the Inhabitants
is broken like the petty Kingdoms in *Africa.*—If we do not join
Heart and Hand in the common Cause against our exulting Foes,
but fall to disputing amongst ourselves, it may really happen as
the Governour of *Pennsylvania* told his Assembly, 'We shall have
no Priviledge to dispute about, nor Country to dispute in.'—

III. Thirdly, of the Future State of North America.—Here we
find a vast stock of proper Materials for the Art and Ingenuity of

Man to work upon:—Treasures of immense Worth; conceal'd
from the poor ignorant aboriginal Natives! The Curious have
observ'd, that the Progress of Humane Literature (like the Sun)
is from the East to the West; thus, has it travellled thro' *Asia*
and *Europe,* and now is arrived at the Eastern Shore of *America.* As the Coelestial Light of the Gospel was directed here by
the Finger of GOD, it will doubtless, finally drive the long!
long! Night of Heathenish Darkness from *America.*—So Arts
and Sciences will change the Face of Nature in their Tour from
Hence over the Appalachian Mountains to the Western Ocean;
and as they march thro' the vast Desert, the Residence of wild
Beasts will be broken up, and their obscene Howl cease for ever;
—Instead of which, the Stones and Trees will dance together at
the Music of *Orpheus,*—the Rocks will disclose their hidden
Gems,—and the inestimable Treasures of Gold & Silver be broken up. Huge Mountains of Iron Ore are already discovered,
and vast Stores are reserved for future Generations: This Metal
more useful than Gold and Silver, will imploy Millions of
Hands, not only to form the martial Sword, and peaceful Share,
alternately; but an Infinity of Utensils improved in the Exercise
of Art, and Handicraft, amongst Men. Nature thro' all her Works
has sharp'd Authority on this Law, namely. "That all fit Matter
shall be improved to its best Purposes."—Shall not then these
vast Quarries, that teem with mechanic Stone,—those for Structure be piled into great Cities,—and those for Sculpture into
Statues of perpetuate the Honor of renowned Heroes; even those
who shall now save their Country.——*O! Ye unborn Inhabitants of America! Should this Page escape its destin'd Conflagra-
tion at the Year's End, and these Alphabetical Letters remain
legible,—when your Eyes behold the Sun after he has rolled the
Seasons round for two or three Centuries more, you will know
that in Anno Domini 1758, we dream'd of your Times.*

5   FROM   *John L. O'Sullivan*
                      Manifest Destiny

Almost all the ideas that make up this doctrine had been fully formed long before 1845, when O'Sullivan coined the phrase "manifest destiny." It first appeared in his Democratic Review *editorial on the annexation of Texas, which is reprinted below. Although one can largely account for the powerful attraction of the doctrine itself, given a new life since Jefferson's acquisition of the Louisiana Territory and the massive infiltration by American settlers of contiguous foreign-held territories, one cannot easily explain why O'Sullivan's particular phrasing caught on, or why these two words had not been combined earlier. An informed guess would be the increased importance attached to tangible evidence in support of ideals during America's first "scientific" age. In this context, the important word is "manifest," although the idea underlying it—to use but one example—had been conjoined to the metaphysical notion of a special American destiny and mission by Thomas Paine in his* Common Sense, *published on the eve of the American Revolution. Of course, O'Sullivan's literary flair and role as the leading publicist for Manifest Destiny during the expansive 1840s helped to popularize the phrase. O'Sullivan's contribution is the subject of Julius W. Pratt's article "The Origins of 'Manifest Destiny,'"* American Historical Review, XXXII *(July 1927) 795–978.*

Texas is now ours. Already, before these words are written, her Convention has undoubtedly ratified the acceptance, by her Congress, of our proffered invitation into the Union; and made the requisite changes in her already republican form of constitu-

SOURCE. John L. O'Sullivan, unsigned editorial in the *Democratic Review* entitled "Annexation," *XVII* (July and August, 1845) , 5–10.

tion to adopt it to its future federal relations. Her star and her
stripe may already be said to have taken their place in the glorious blazon of our common nationality; and the sweep of our
eagle's wing already includes within its circuit the wide extent of
her fair and fertile land. She is no longer to us a mere geographical space—a certain combination of coast, plain, mountain, valley, forest and stream. She is no longer to us a mere country on
the map. She comes within the dear and sacred designation of
Our Country; no longer a *"pays,"* she is a part of *"la patrie;"*
and that which is at once a sentiment and a virtue, Patriotism,
already begins to thrill for her too within the national heart. It is
time then that all should cease to treat her as alien, and even ad-
verse—cease to denounce and vilify all and everything connected
with her accession—cease to thwart and oppose the remaining
steps for its consummation; or where such efforts are felt to be
unavailing, at least to embitter the hour of reception by all the
most ungracious frowns of aversion and words of unwelcome.
There has been enough of all this. It has had its fitting day during the period when, in common with every other possible question of practical policy that can arise, it unfortunately became
one of the leading topics of party division, of presidential elec-
tioneering. But that period has passed, and with it let its prejudices and its passions, its discords and its denunciations, pass
away too. The next session of Congress will see the representatives of the new young State in their places in both our halls of
national legislation, side by side with those of the old Thirteen.
Let their reception into "the family" be frank, kindly, and cheerful, as befits such an occasion, as comports not less with our own
selfrespect than patriotic duty towards them. Ill betide those foul
birds that delight to 'file their own nest, and disgust the ear with
perpetual discord of ill-omened croak.

Why, were other reasoning wanting, in favor of now elevating
this question of the reception of Texas into the Union, out of the
lower region of our past party dissensions, up to its proper level
of a high and broad nationality, it surely is to be found, found
abundantly, in the manner in which other nations have undertaken to intrude themselves into it, between us and the proper
parties to the case, in a spirit of hostile interference against us,

for the avowed object of thwarting our policy and hampering our power, limiting our greatness and checking the fulfilment of our *manifest destiny** to overspread the continent allotted by Providence for the free development of our yearly multiplying millions. This we have seen done by England, our old rival and enemy; and by France, strangely coupled with her against us, under the influence of the Anglicism strongly tinging the policy of her present prime minister, Guizot. The zealous activity with which this effort to defeat us was pushed by the representatives of those governments, together with the character of intrigue accompanying it, fully constituted that case of foreign interference, which Mr. Clay himself declared should, and would unite us all in maintaining the common cause of our country against the foreigner and the foe. . . .

It is wholly untrue, and unjust to ourselves, the pretence that the Annexation has been a measure of spoliation, unrightful and unrighteous—of military conquest under forms of peace and law —of territorial aggrandizement at the expense of justice, and justice due by a double sanctity to the weak. This view of the question is wholly unfounded, and has been before so amply refuted in these pages, as well as in a thousand other modes, that we shall not again dwell upon it. The independence of Texas was complete and absolute. It was an independence, not only in fact but of right. No obligation of duty towards Mexico tended in the least degree to restrain our right to effect the desired recovery of the fair province once our own—whatever motives of policy might have prompted a more deferential consideration of her feelings and her pride, as involved in the question. If Texas became peopled with an American population, it was by no contrivance of our government, but on the express invitation of that of Mexico herself; accompanied with such guaranties of State independence, and the maintenance of a federal system analogous to our own, as constituted a compact fully justifying the strongest measures of redress on the part of those afterwards deceived in this guaranty, and sought to be enslaved under the yoke imposed by its violation. She was released, rightfully and absolutely released, from all Mexican allegiance, or duty of cohesion to the

* Italics are the present editor's.

Mexican political body, by the acts and fault of Mexico herself, and Mexico alone. There never was a clearer case. It was not revolution; it was resistance to revolution; and resistance under such circumstances as left independence the necessary resulting state, caused by the abandonment of those with whom her former federal association had existed. What then can be more preposterous than all this clamor by Mexico and the Mexican interest, against Annexation, as a violation of any rights of hers, any duties of ours? . . .

Nor is there any just foundation for the charge that Annexation is a great pro-slavery measure—calculated to increase and perpetuate that institution. Slavery had nothing to do with it. Opinions were and are greatly divided, both at the North and South, as to the influence to be exerted by it on Slavery and the Slave States. That it will tend to facilitate and hasten the disappearance of Slavery from all the northern tier of the present Slave States, cannot surely admit of serious question. The greater value in Texas of the slave labor now employed in those States, must soon produce the effect of draining off that labor southwardly, by the same unvarying law that bids water descend the slope that invites it. Every new Slave State in Texas will make at least one Free State from among those in which that institution now exists—to say nothing of those portions of Texas on which slavery cannot spring and grow—to say nothing of the far more rapid growth of new States in the free West and Northwest, as these fine regions are overspread by the emigration fast flowing over them from Europe, as well as from the Northern and Eastern States of the Union as it exists. On the other hand, it is undeniably much gained for the cause of the eventual voluntary abolition of slavery, that it should have been thus drained off towards the only outlet which appeared to furnish much probability of the ultimate disappearance of the negro race from our borders. The Spanish-Indian-American populations of Mexico, Central America and South America, afford the only receptacle capable of absorbing that race whenever we shall be prepared to slough it off—to emancipate it from slavery, and (simultaneously necessary) to remove it from the midst of our own. Themselves already of mixed and confused blood, and free from the "prejudices" which among us so insuperably forbid the social amalgamation which can alone elevate the Negro race out of a virtually servile degradation even though legally free, the regions occupied by those populations must strongly attract the black race in that direction; and as soon as the destined hour of emancipation shall arrive, will relieve the question of one of its worst difficulties, if not absolutely the greatest.

No—Mr. Clay was right when he declared that Annexation was a question with which slavery had nothing to do. The country which was the subject of Annexation in this case, from its geographical position and relations, happens to be—or rather the portion of it now actually settled, happens to be—a slave country. But a similar process might have taken place in proximity to a different section of our Union; and indeed there is a great deal of Annexation yet to take place, within the life of the present generation, along the whole line of our northern border. Texas has been absorbed into the Union in the inevitable fulfilment of the general law which is rolling our population westward; the connexion of which with that ratio of growth in population which is destined within a hundred years to swell our numbers to the enormous population of *two hundred and fifty millions* (if not more), is too evident to leave us in doubt of the manifest design of Providence in regard to the occupation of this continent. It was disintegrated from Mexico in the natural course of events, by a process perfectly legitimate on its own part, blameless on ours; and in which all the censures due to wrong, perfidy and folly, rest on Mexico alone. And possessed as it was by a population which was in truth but a colonial detachment from our own, and which was still bound by myriad ties of the very heartstrings to its old relations, domestic and political, their incorporation into the Union was not only inevitable, but the most natural, right and proper thing in the world—and it is only astonishing that there should be any among ourselves to say it nay. . . . With no friendship for slavery, though unprepared to excommunicate to eternal damnation, with bell, book, and candle, those who are, we see nothing in the bearing of the Annexation of Texas on that institution to awaken a doubt of the wisdom of that measure, or a compunction for the humble part contributed by us towards its consummation.

California will, probably, next fall away from the loose adhesion which, in such a country as Mexico, holds a remote province in a slight equivocal kind of dependence on the metropolis. Imbecile and distracted, Mexico never can exert any real governmental authority over such a country. The impotence of the one and the distance of the other, must make the relation one of virtual independence; unless, by stunting the province of all natural growth, and forbidding that immigration which can alone develope its capabilities and fulfil the purposes of its creation, tyranny may retain a military dominion which is no government in the legitimate sense of the term. In the case of California this is now impossible. The Anglo-Saxon foot is already on its borders. Already the advance guard of the irresistible army of Anglo-Saxon emigration has begun to pour down upon it, armed with the plough and the rifle, and marking its trail with schools and colleges, courts and representative halls, mills and meeting-houses. A population will soon be in actual occupation of California, over which it will be idle for Mexico to dream of dominion. They will necessarily become independent. All this without agency of our government, without responsibility of our people —in the natural flow of events, the spontaneous working of principles, and the adaptation of the tendencies and wants of the human race to the elemental circumstances in the midst of which they find themselves placed. And they will have a right to independence—to self-government—to the possession of the homes conquered from the wilderness by their own labors and dangers, sufferings and sacrifices—a better and a truer right than the artificial title of sovereignty in Mexico a thousand miles distant, inheriting from Spain a title good only against those who have none better. Their right to independence will be the natural right of self-government belonging to any community strong enough to maintain it—distinct in position, origin and character, and free from any mutual obligations of membership of a common political body, binding it to others by the duty of loyalty and compact of public faith. This will be their title to independence; and by this title, there can be no doubt that the population now fast streaming down upon California will both assert and maintain that independence. Whether they will then attach themselves to our Union or not, is not to be predicted with any certainty. Unless the projected rail-road across the continent to the Pacific be carried into effect, perhaps they may not; though even in that case, the day is not distant when the Empires of the Atlantic and Pacific would again flow together into one, as soon as their inland border should approach each other. But that great work, colossal as appears the plan on its first suggestion, cannot remain long unbuilt. Its necessity for this very purpose of binding and holding together in its iron clasp our fast settling Pacific region with that of the Mississippi valley—the natural facility of the route—the ease with which any amount of labor for the construction can be drawn in from the overcrowded populations of Europe, to be paid in the lands made valuable by the progress of the work itself—and its immense utility to the commerce of the world with the whole eastern coast of Asia, alone almost sufficient for the support of such a road—these considerations give assurance that the day cannot be distant which shall witness the conveyance of the representatives from Oregon and California to Washington within less time than a few years ago was devoted to a similar journey by those from Ohio; while the magnetic telegraph will enable the editors of the "San Francisco Union," the "Astoria Evening Post," or the "Nootka Morning News" to set up in type the first half of the President's Inaugural, before the echoes of the latter half shall have died away beneath the lofty porch of the Capitol, as spoken from his lips.

Away, then, with all idle French talk of *balances of power* on the American Continent. There is no growth in Spanish America! Whatever progress of population there may be in the British Canadas, is only for their own early severance of their present colonial relation to the little island three thousand miles across the Atlantic; soon to be followed by Annexation, and destined to swell the still accumulating momentum of our progress. And whosoever may hold the balance, though they should cast into the opposite scale all the bayonets and cannon, not only of France and England, but of Europe entire, how would it kick the beam against the simple solid weight of the two hundred and fifty, or three hundred millions—and American millions—destined to gather beneath the flutter of the stripes and stars, in the fast hastening year of the Lord 1945!

6 FROM   *Anonymous*
   Manifest Destiny—A Rendezvous for Rogues

*The following short piece is notable for its tone of studied am-
bivalence, setting it apart from the ardent expansionist sentiment
that characterized Californians during the 1840s and 1850s. It is
very possible, of course, that critical remarks were slipped into
the original text by a publishing house editor in New York. And
yet native Californians were capable of self-criticism, as indicat-
ed by Josiah Royce's account of "Squatter's Rights and Manifest
Destiny," reprinted in* C. Merton Babcock, editor, The American Frontier: A Social and Literary Record *(New York and San
Francisco: Holt, Rinehart and Winston, Inc., 1965), pp. 224–231.*

It is the fate of America ever to "go ahead." She is like the rod
of Aaron that became a serpent and swallowed up the other rods.
So will America conquer or annex all lands. That is her "manifest destiny." Only give her time for the process. To swallow up
every few years a province as large as most European kingdoms
is her present rate of progress. Sometimes she purchases the
mighty morsel, sometimes she forms it out of waste territory by
the natural increase of her own people, sometimes she "annex-
es," and sometimes she conquers it. Her progress is still steadily
onward. Pioneers clear the way. These are political agents with
money bags, or settlers in neglected parts of the continent, or
peaceable American citizens who happen to reside in the desired
countries, and who wish to dwell under the old "Stars and
Stripes," or they may be only proper filibusters, who steal and
fight gratuitously for their own fast-following Uncle Sam. When
they fail in their schemes they are certainly scoundrels, and are

SOURCE. *The Annals of San Francisco,* by Soule, Gihon and Nisbet (New
York, 1855) , n. p.

commonly so termed; when they succeed, though they be dubbed heroes, they are still the old rogues. Meanwhile AMERICA (that is the true title of our country) secures the spoils won to her hand, however dishonestly they may have come. That is only her destiny, and perhaps she is not so blameable as a nation in bearing it willingly. One may profit by the treason, yet hate the traitor. America must round her territories by the sea.

PART TWO

Continental Expansion

QUOTABLE QUOTES

"Another thing that seemeth probable to me, is, that the *New-English* Planters were the Forerunners of the King of the East; and as the Morning Star, giving certain Intelligence that the Sun of Righteousness will quickly rise and Shine with Illustrious Grace and Favour, upon this despised Hemisphere."

Samuel Sewall, 1697

" 'Tis time to part.' . . . The time likewise at which the continent was discovered, adds weight to the argument, and the manner in which it was peopled increases the force of it. The Reformation was preceded by the discovery of America, as if the Almighty graciously meant to open a sanctuary to the persecuted in future years. . ."

Thomas Paine, 1776

"[W]e have an immensity of land courting the industry of the husbandman. . . . Those who labor in the earth are the chosen people of God, if ever He had a chosen people, whose breasts He has made His peculiar deposit of substantial and genuine virtue."

Thomas Jefferson, 1782

"It is not imaginable that, in the present condition of the world, *any* European nation should entertain the project of settling a *colony* on the Northwestern Coast of America; that the United States should form establishments there, with views of absolute territorial right and inland commerce, is not only to be expected, but is pointed out by the finger of nature" . . .

John Quincy Adams, 1823

"[America] is the country of the Future. From Washington, proverbially 'the city of magnificent distances,' through all its cities, states, and territories, it is a country of beginnings, of projects, of designs, of expectations. Gentlemen, there is a subline and friendly Destiny by which the human race is guided. . ."

Ralph Waldo Emerson, 1844

"It is not a little amusing to observe what different views are taken as to the indications of 'the hand of nature' and the pointings of 'the finger of God,' by the same gentleman, under different circumstances and upon different subjects. In one quarter of the compass they can descry the hand of nature in a level desert and a second-rte river, beckoning us impatiently to march up to them. But when they turn their eyes to another part of the horizon, the loftiest mountains in the universe are quite lost upon their gaze. There is no hand of nature there. The configuration of the earth has no longer any significance. The Rocky Mountains are mere molehills. Our destiny is onward."

Robert C. Winthrop, 1844

7 FROM   *John Robinson*
The Cause of Heaven in Mexico

*Little is known of Dr. John Robinson, except that he served
with Zebulon Pike's expedition to New Mexico in 1806 to 1807
and that he died many years later in Mexico, a martyr to the
cause of independence for Hispanic America. The crisis to which
he refers in this pamphlet had to do with the Napoleonic wars in
Europe and the War of 1812. At this time of universal unrest,
Robinson thought he saw an opportunity to promote revolutionary sympathies while striking a death blow to traditional American enemies. Napoleon's subjugation of Spain in 1811 had given
birth to a strong independence movement in Latin America,
which Robinson feared might be taken over, in the absence of
American aid, by Great Britain. At the very moment he was
writing this pamphlet, American armed forces were descending
on Canada with reasonable assurances of success. His visionary
friend, General Zebulon Pike, had recently been killed in an
otherwise successful raid on Toronto, and another friend, General
John Wilkinson, was advancing on Montreal.*

*This pamphlet must be read, however, in the light of Aaron
Burr's alleged plot earlier to carve an independent Yankee em-*

SOURCE. Robinson's *Broadside* (Philadelphia, 1813) , reprinted in *The Journals of Zebulon Montgomery Pike,* edited by Donald Jackson (Norman,
Oklahoma, 1966) , *II,* 382–387.

*pire out of Mexico, for the two men whom Robinson most ad-
mired, Pike and Wilkinson, were charged with complicity in
Burr's project. Most of the ideas in this pamphlet stem from
Pike, who received exoneration from the then-Secretary of War,
with the blessings of President Jefferson. This pamphlet, published in 1813, contains the earliest expression we have of Manifest Destiny doctrine within a national context of geographical
expansion. The same ambiguity about imperialistic designs at-
taches to it as have accompanied the Burr trial and the continuing scholarly controversy about Manifest Destiny, for Robinson
couples an ideal national interest with notions of selfish gain. It
seems to follow (or lead) a pattern of American expansion
wherein the flag is officially innocent. In any event, the major
thrust of Manifest Destiny was westward. Special attention in
this pamphlet should be paid to Robinson's argument for a
kindred interest between citizens of the United States and Latin
America, because later documents argue the reverse: that Latin
Indian peoples cannot be assimilated to American culture.*

PHILADELPHIA Sept. 16th 1813

Confidential
FELLOW CITIZEN

We now witness the most momentous crisis, which the history
of man has ever furnished, on the review of which, the mind is
filled with awfully solemn reflections; turning our attention to the
East, we behold all Europe laid waste, we behold her plains red-
dened with the blood of her innocent inhabitants: The fate of
kingdoms and empires is at this moment suspended by mere
threads, even the shores of Columbia are now whitened with the
tents of armies; our ears are assailed on all sides by the din of
camps, the sound of martial music, the cries of suffering humanity and the mournful sound of Peace retiring from this Globe.

This, then, is the moment when the patriotism, nay the very
souls of Americans are to be tried. Awake! Arise my fellow citizen! Shake from you this stupor, step forth, defend the rights

and liberties of your country, and aid in establishing, on a noble
and widely extended basis, those principles of Republicanism,
which shall secure to our beloved country her future peace, tran-
quility and Independence.

It is evident that our Government requires but a small portion
of her active young men in the present contest with Great Britain, and it is equally evident that there are many thousands of
noble, brave and enterprising men whose chief desire is to distinguish themselves in the service which shall go to establish on a
solid foundation the liberties of Americans, and the Independence of this continent; in consideration therefore, of the high respect which I entertain for your patriotism, valour and fidelity, I
have conceived it my duty, to call your attention to the Mexican
revolution, as a subject peculiarly interesting to the future welfare of this republic, and the future prosperity of her citizens.

Fellow citizen, whether a Bourbon, Braganza or a Bonaparte
reigns in the peninsula of Spain, is of very little importance to us,
but on crossing the atlantic this revolution changes its character,
as it relates to the United States, and involves in its course their
future peace, prosperity and even Independence. The Spanish
government feeling their incapacity to suppress that revolution,
have applied to their ally, who has by treaty, agreed to mediate
between the insurgent provinces and their metropolis, and even-
tually for a valuable consideration, to gaurantee the integrity of
the Spanish monarchy on this continent: it is not necessary here
to calculate the ability of Great Britain to fulfill the conditions of
this treaty, it is sufficient for our purpose to know that a government who has subjugated India and openly aspires to the *exclu-
sive commerce of the world,* has made such a contract; but the
revolution in Mexico has gone too far for mediation, consequently British bayonets would have to be employed to reduce and
disarm the insurgents, and when that revolution is thus quelled,
who will be the real masters of that country? will any man pre-
sume to say, that the imbecile government of Spain will have any
authority there? No, a British General will dictate laws to, and
control the destinies of Mexico, and to suppose that then, the resources of New Spain would not be turned against the United
States, would be extravagant indeed: it is well known that even

at this moment a great portion of the wealth of that country passes into the coffers of Great Britain, and is consequently turned against this government.

The best authorities shew the population of Mexico to be 5,999,300 souls, who are distinguished by the following divisions, viz. Europeans 74,000; Creole 1,010,000; mixed Breed 2,595,000; domiciliated Indians, 2,320,200. This numerous people are spread over an immense country, bounded on the South and East by the Isthmus of Darrin, the bays of Nicaragua, Honduras and Mexico. On the East and North, by the ancient province of Louisiana, and on the West, by the Pacific ocean.

This envied region surpasses all others in natural advantages, the country gradually rises from both oceans, until it attains a temperature of climate that seems to be the most favorable to the nature of man; in the elevated plains, the soil is exuberantly fertile and peculiarly adapted to the production of all the fruits, grass and vegetables, necessary to his wants and luxuries. It is also peculiarly proper for rearing domestic animals, for they are found there better in their species and more abundant than in any other country; and there may be produced every article of raw material for manufacturing, that we are acquainted with from the Torrid to the Temperate Zone, in sufficient abundance to supply the workshops of all Europe. Mexico is the capital, and is one of the finest cities in the world, it is situated at about an equal distance from the two oceans, and enjoys the singular advantage of at the same time giving the hand to the United States and Europe on the one side, and from the other communicating with Asia. The wealth of Mexico in minerals is even proverbial. She furnishes a great proportion of the precious metals to the world, the revenue of the Crown, heretofore, may be estimated at $16,800,000 per annum.

Such, Sir, is New Spain, she is our nearest neighbour, and may become an useful friend, or an inconvenient, even a dangerous enemy, according to the policy we persue towards her, at this critical juncture. In this interesting country a revolution now rages with circumstances of violence and public misery, almost without a parallel in history, unless it be found in the wars of Cortes or Pizarro.

The Royal army amounts to 60,000 men, and are scattered

over their possessions in the Vice Royalty and interior provinces to prevent the people from rising to assert their rights, consequently they cannot be embodied, without the most fatal consequences to the interest of their cause.

The Republican armies amount to about 40,000 men, and have been able to maintain their ground in the field for the three last years, they at present occupy nearly one half of the territories of New Spain, and ere long must be free; a people who rise in vindication of their violated rights, and are able to withstand the torrent of constituted and arbitrary authorities, for that length of time, become invincible.

They have established foundries, and have even taken many of the bells from the churches to make cannon, they have also manufactured some small arms but for want of a sufficient number of good armorers, and the proper materials, they have not been able to make any considerable progress in that branch. They manufacture their own powder, and lead is found in great abundance in that country. The clergy of New Spain are generally in favour of the revolution, it was they, who gave that revolution its first impulse, and they continue to support it, some of them, even put on the sword and head the armies in the field.

The Mexican, in character, is mild, affable, polite, hospitable and gay, they possess great fortitude, no privation, however great, will cause a murmur; in fine they are as good materials for an army, as have ever come within my view; they require nothing but discipline, to render them as good troops as any in the world.

The character of the citizens of the United States, stands preeminently high in that country, and they will receive them with the most fraternal affection, they very justly perceive that we have a common interest, and therefore ought to be friends.

The late gallant and brave General Pike (who would have been with us, had he lived,) observes, in his journal, in speaking on this subject in an official letter: "I yet possess immense matter, the result of one years travels through a country desert and populated, which have both been long the subject of curiosity to the philosopher, the anxious desire of the miser, and the waking thoughts and sleeping dreams of the man of ambition and the aspiring soul: And in our present critical situation, I do conceive immensely important, and which opens a scene for the generosity and aggrandisement of our country, with a wide and splendid field for harvests of honor and profit to individuals": and in the same work he observes, "It would be requisite that not only the General commanding, but every officer down to the youngest ensign should be impressed with the necessity of supporting a strict discipline. The most sacred regard should be paid not to injure the institution of their Religion: thereby showing them we had a proper respect for all things in any way connected with the worship of the Deity, and at the same time we permitted every man to adore him agreeably to the dictates of his own judgment. Should an army of Americans ever march into that country, and be guided and governed by these maxims, they will only have to march from province to province, and be hailed by the united voices of grateful millions as their deliverers and saviors, whilst our national character, would be resounded, to the most distant nations of the Earth."

Fellow Citizen, there is no country in the world which presents so noble and glorious a field for men of mi-[*one or two words missing*] or such immense prospects of wealth to the enterprising merchant, nor is there a country on earth in [which] there is so great a certainty of independent fortunes for the gentlemen of professions and trades.

I write to you my fellow citizen, to accompany me in that glorious and brilliant course, which heaven has marked [for] you and your countrymen. There, six millions of souls, who for these three hundred years have been borne down by the yoke of a cruel oppression, rise and demand the restoration of their long lost rights and offer their [*one word missing*] orisons to heaven and you for assistance. Arise my fellow citizen! can you longer remain an unfeeling [spectator] of this grand and interesting spectacle, Arise! lead on a few of your countrymen, such as are distinguished by talents and virtues, the eyes of your country and all Europe are on you, and ere long you shall hear the plaudits of an admiring and grateful world, hailing that immortal Band, and the entrance of the Mexican Republic, into the sublime rank of civilized nations.

Health and Fraternity,
JOHN H. ROBINSON

8 FROM   *Thomas Hart Benton*
               America's Pathway to the Orient

*Frequently reprinted and anthologized, this Senate speech by
the "Magnificent Missourian" typifies Manifest Destiny at its eloquent best, and it offers readers an unusual opportunity by
means of textual analysis to weigh for themselves the relative
strength of the various motives which have influenced American
expansion. For Benton could be considered without great exag-
geration Mr. Manifest Destiny. The larger views presented here,
for instance, were to echo on the floor of the United States Senate during the great debates on the acquisition of the Philippines
following the Spanish-American War as expressed by Albert J.
Beveridge and Henry Cabot Lodge. On the basis of this speech
alone, one might question the widely accepted interpretation of-
fered by Professor Merk that imperialism "was the antithesis of
Manifest Destiny. Manifest Destiny was continentalism."*

. . . [Oregon] is valuable, both as a country to be inhabited,
and as a position to be held and defended. I speak of it, first, as
a position, commanding the North Pacific ocean, and overlook-
ing the eastern coast of India. The North Pacific is a rich sea,
and is already the seat of a great commerce: British, French,
American, Russian, and ships of other nations, frequent it. Our
whaling ships cover it: our ships of war go there to protect our
interests; and, great as that interest now is, it is only the beginning. Futurity will develop an immense, and various, commerce
on that sea, of which the far greater part will be American. That
commerce, neither in the merchant ships which carry it on, nor
in the military marine which protects it, can find a port, to call

SOURCE. Benton's *Speech on the Oregon Question: Delivered in the Senate
of the United States May 22, 25, and 28, 1846* (Washington, D. C., 1846),
passim.

its own, within twenty thousand miles of the field of its operations. The double length of the two Americas has to be run—a stormy and tempestuous cape to be doubled—to find itself in a port of its own country: while here lies one in the very edge of its field, ours by right, ready for use, and ample for every purpose of refuge and repair, protection and domination. Can we turn our back upon it? and, in turning the back, deliver it up to the British? Insane, and suicidal would be the fatal act! . . .

Agriculturally the value of the country is great; . . .

Commercially, the advantages of Oregon will be great—far greater than any equal portion of the Atlantic States. The eastern Asiatics, who will be their chief customer, are more numerous than our customers in western Europe—more profitable to trade with, and less dangerous to quarrel with. Their articles of commerce are richer than those of Europe; they want what the Oregons will have to spare—bread and provisions—and have no systems of policy to prevent them from purchasing these necessaries of life from those who can supply them. The sea which washes their shores is every way a better sea than the Atlantic —richer in its whale and other fisheries—in the fur regions which enclose it to the north—more fortunate in the tranquillity of its character, in its freedom from storms, gulf-streams, and icebergs—in its perfect adaptation to steam navigation—in its intermediate or half-way islands, and its myriad of rich islands on its further side;—in its freedom from maritime Powers on its coasts, except the American, which is to grow up at the mouth of the Columbia. As a people to trade with—as a sea to navigate —the Mongolian race of eastern Asia, and the North Pacific ocean, are far preferable to the Europeans and the Atlantic. . . .

GOD'S CHOSEN PEOPLE

The effect of the arrival of the Caucasian, or White race, on the western coast of America, opposite the eastern coast of Asia, remains to be mentioned among the benefits which the settlement of the Columbia will produce, and that a benefit, not local to us, but general and universal to the human race. Since the dispersion of man upon earth, I know of no human event, past or present, which promises a greater, and more beneficent change upon earth than the arrival of the van of the Caucasian race (the Celtic-Anglo-Saxon division) upon the border of the sea which washes the shore of the eastern Asia. The Mongolian, or Yellow race, is there, four hundred millions in number, spreading almost to Europe; a race once the foremost of the human family in the arts of civilization, but torpid and stationary for thousands of years. It is a race far above the Ethiopian, or Black—above the Malay, or Brown, (if we must admit five races) —and above the American Indian, or Red: it is a race far above all these, but still, far below the White; and like all the rest, must receive an impresion from the superior race whenever they come in contact. It would seem that the White race alone received the divine command, to subdue and replenish the earth! for it is the only race that has obeyed it—the only one that hunts out new and distant lands, and even a New World, to subdue and replenish. Starting from western Asia, taking Europe for their field, and the Sun for their guide, and leaving the Mongolians behind, they arrived, after many ages, on the shores of the Atlantic, which they lit up with the lights of science and religion, and adorned with the useful and the elegant arts. Three and a half centuries ago, this race, in obedience to the great command, arrived in the New World, and found new lands to subdue and replenish. For a long time, it was confined to the border of the new field, (I now mean the Celtic-Anglo-Saxon division;) and even fourscore years ago the philosophic Burke was considered a rash man because he said the English colonists would top the Alleghanies, and descend into the valley of the Mississippi, and occupy without parchment if the Crown refused to make grants of land. What was considered a rash declaration eighty years ago, is old history, in our young country, at this day. Thirty years ago I said the same thing of the Rocky Mountains and the Columbia: it was ridiculed then: it is becoming history to-day. The venerable Mr. Macon has often told me that he remembered a line low down in North Carolina, fixed by a royal governor as a boundary between the whites and the Indians: where is that boundary now?

The van of the Caucasian race now top the Rocky Mountains, and spread down to the shores of the Pacific. In a few years a great population will grow up there, luminous with the accumulated lights of European and American civilization. Their presence in such a position cannot be without its influence upon eastern Asia. The sun of civilization must shine across the sea: socially and commercially, the van of the Caucasians, and the rear of the Mongolians, must intermix. They must talk together, and trade together, and marry together. Commerce is a great civilizer —social intercourse as great—and marriage greater. The White and Yellow races can marry together, as well as eat and trade together. Moral and intellectual superiority will do the rest: the White race will take the ascendant, elevating what is susceptible of improvement—wearing out what is not. The Red race has disappeared from the Atlantic coast: the tribes that resisted civilization, met extinction. This is a cause of lamentation with many. For my part, I cannot murmur at what seems to be the effect of divine law. I cannot repine that this Capitol has replaced the wigwam—this Christian people, replaced the savages—white matrons, the red squaws—and that such men as Washington, Franklin, and Jefferson, have taken the place of Powhattan, Opechonecanough, and other red men, howsoever respectable they may have been as savages. Civilization, or extinction, has been the fate of all people who have found themselves in the track of the advancing Whites, and civilization, always the preference of the Whites, has been pressed as an object, while extinction has followed as a consequence of its resistance. The Black and the Red races have often felt their ameliorating influence. The Yellow race, next to themselves in the scale of mental and moral excellence, and in the beauty of form, once their superiors in the useful and elegant arts, and in learning, and still respectable though stationary; this race cannot fail to receive a new impulse from the approach of the Whites, improved so much since so many ages ago they left the western borders of Asia. The apparition of the van of the Caucasian race, rising upon them in the east after having left them on the west, and after having completed the circumnavigation of the globe, must wake up and reanimate the torpid body of old Asia. Our position and policy will commend us to their hospitable reception: political considerations will aid the action of social and commercial influences. Pressed upon by the great Powers of Europe—the same that press upon us—they must in our approach see the advent of friends, not of foes—of benefactors, not of invaders. The moral and intellectual superiority of the White race will do the rest: and thus, the youngest people, and the newest land, will become the reviver and the regenerator of the oldest.

It is in this point of view, and as acting upon the social, political, and religious condition of Asia, and giving a new point of departure to her ancient civilization, that I look upon the settlement of the Columbia river by the van of the Caucasian race as the most momentous human event in the history of man since his dispersion over the face of the earth. . . .

9 FROM   *"Vox Populi"*
          For Texas and for Oregon

Language breaks into poetry and song when emotions are stirred. The major poet of Manifest Destiny was Walt Whitman. Major literary figures who warmed in varous ways to westward dreaming include William Cullen Bryant, Ralph Waldo Emerson, Henry David Thoreau, Edgar Allen Poe, and Herman Melville. The Mexican War was, for the most part, anathema to these dreamers, as exemplified by James Russell Lowell's Biglow Papers *and Thoreau's* Civil Disobedience. *The following selections suggest not only that they did not well represent the great American public but that the Oregon and Texas agitation transcended sectional interests. This perhaps deservedly forgotten body of literature hews closely to continentalism.*

SOURCE. William McCarty, compiler, *National Songs, Ballads, and other Patriotic Poetry Chiefly Relating to the War of 1846* (Philadelphia, 1846), pp. 35–38, 65–66, 88–89, 99–100.

SONG OF THE VOLUNTEERS

BY OUR JONATHAN

(Tune—"Old Dan Tucker")

The Mexicans are on our soil,
In war they wish us to embroil;
They've tried their best and worst to vex us
By murdering our brave men in Texas.
    Chorus—We're on our way to Rio Grande,
                On our way to Rio Grande,
                on our way to Rio Grande,
                And with arms they'll find us handy.

We are the boys who fear no noise,
We'll leave behind us all our joys
To punish those half-savage scamps,
Who've slain our brethren in their camps.
    Chorus—We're on our way to Matamoras,
                On our way to Matamoras,
                On our Way to Matamoras,
                And we'll drive them all before us.

They've slaughtered Porter, Kain and Cross—
Most deeply we deplore their loss—
Those bloody deeds we'll make them rue
And pay them off for old and new!
        We're on our way to Matamoras, &c.

We'll cross the famous Rio Grande,
Engage the villains hand to hand,
And punish them for all their sins
By stripping off their yellow skins.
        We're on our way, &c.

Herrera and Paredes too,
And all the chiefs of the vile crew
We'll show unto their lazzaroni
Mounted on a wooden pony
        We're on our way, &c.

And when we've punished them enough
We'll make them shell us out the stuff,
To pay the war's expense, and then
We'll have, besides, old Yucatan!
  We're on our way, &c.

Meanwhile our brethren in the west
Will for our nation do their best,
And when they've ended their long journey
Our flag will float in California.
  We're on our way, &c.

The world is wide, our views are large,
We're sailing on in Freedom's barge,
Our God is good and we are brave,
From tyranny the world we'll save.
  We're on our way, &c.

We have a mission to fulfil,
And every drop of blood we'll spill,
Unless the tyrants of our race
Come quail before our eagle's face.
  We're on our way, &c.

He is thrice armed whose quarrel's just,
And we fight now because we must,
And any force that would us stop,
Down to the earth must surely drop.
  We're on our way, &c.

John Bull may meddle if he please,
But he had better keep at ease,
For we are strong by sea and land—
If he don't mind we'll have old Ireland!
  We're on our way, &c.

So every honest volunteer
May now come forth—the coast is clear;
We ask no odds, but we are bent
On having this whole continent.
  We're on our way, &c.

We go for equal rights and laws,
We'll bravely fight in Freedom's cause,
And though the world may take the field,
To tyrants we will never yield.
            We're on our way, &c.

The God of War, the mighty Mars,
Has smiled upon our stripes and stars;
And spite of any ugly rumors
We'll vanquish all the Montezumas!
            We're on our way to Matamoras,
            On our way to Matamoras,
            On our way to Matamoras,
            And we'll conquer all before us!

OUR COUNTRY

BY J. W. PEABODY

Our country! 'tis a glorious land—
    With broad arms stretched from shore to shore;
The proud Pacific chafes her strand,
    She hears the dark Atlantic's roar;
And nurtured in her ample breast,
    How many a goodly prospect lies
In Nature's wildest grandeur drest.

Rich prairies decked with flowers of gold,
    Like sun-lit ocean roll afar;
Broad lakes her azure heavens behold,
    Reflecting clear each trembling star;
And mighty rivers, mountain born,
    Go sweeping onward, dark and deep,
Through forests, where the bounding fawn
    Beneath their sheltering branches leap.

And cradled 'mid her clustering hills,
    Sweet lakes in dreamlike beauty hide,
Where love, the air with music fills,
    And calm content and Peace abide;

For Plenty here her fullness pours,
  In rich profusion o'er the land,
And sent to seize her generous stores,
  There prowls no tyrant's hireling band.

Great God! we thank Thee for this home,
  This bounteous birth-land of the Free,
Where wanderers from afar may come,
  And breathe the air of Liberty;
Still may her flowers untrammelled spring,
  Her harvests wave, her cities rise;
And yet, till time shall fold his wing,
  Remain Earth's loveliest Paradise!

FOR TEXAS AND FOR OREGON

(Tune—"Dandy Jim")

Columbia's mighty flag of Mars,
Has gained two bright and glowing stars,
But foemen jealous of their light,
To pluck their glories now unite.
  Be ready then to strike the blow,
  Gainst Johnny Bull or Mexico,
  Arm for the field both sire and son,
  For Texas and for Oregon.

Each spot bold lads, is all our own,
'Twas cultured by our sons alone,
By freemen's hands that soil was till'd,
And fremen's hands shall hold it still.
  Be ready then to strike the blow, &c.

Our sons upon each spot so free,
First planted freedom's holy tree,
They nourished it with blood and toil,
And have the first right to the soil.
  Be ready then to strike the blow, &c.

Let freedom's pioneers still find,
That Uncle Sam walks close behind,

And each spot where their flag's unfurl'd,
He will defend against the world.
  Be ready then to strike, &c.

Let Mexico and Bull unite,
To rob us of our holy right,
We'll fire annexation's gun,
And sweep off ev'ry hostile son.
  Be ready then to strike, &c.

Each mountain steram shall like a flood,
Run purple with the foeman's blood,
Who from our holy flag would tear,
The two young stars we've woven there.
  Be ready then to strike, &c.

SONG OF THE SETTLERS OF OREGON

(Tune—"Sing Darkies Sing")

Out, out, pilgrims out,
  Rend the air with freedom's shout,
Out, out, pilgrims' out,
  For our soil of Oregon.

'Ere Britons own the ground we till
Our dearest blood we'll freely spill,
Till Oregon shines pure and free,
A star in freedom's galaxy.
    Out, out, pilgrims out, &c.

Our prairie flowers,
  First sown by freedom's hand,
Our noble rivers,
  By freemen's eyes first scanned,
Our lofty mountains,
  By freemen first explored,
Shall be defended,
  By freedom's gleaming sword.
    Out, out, pilgrims out, &c.

The sea alone shall be the line,
To make Columbia's right divine,
And California and Canada,
Shall yield to freedom's happy sway.

    Out, out, pilgrims out,
    Rend the air with freedom's shout,
    Out, out, freemen out,
      For our homes in Oregon.

10 FROM *William Walker*
Shall the Western World Be European or American?

William Walker (1824–1860), lawyer, doctor, and journalist, was king of American filibuster, *a word originally applied to territorial adventuring, of which an early forerunner was Dr. John Robinson. After an unsuccessful filibustering expedition into Lower California in 1853, he addressed himself wholeheartedly to the project of realizing a canal across the Isthmus in competition with the projectors of a transcontinental railroad. Although the California gold rush initially forced the question of such transit into prominence and although Walker received important backing from United States isthmian-transit commercial interests, this "grey-eyed man of destiny" was primarily interested in promoting a mystic dream of America as the carrier of a superior civilization from east to west. As such, he anticipated the popular rationale for the acquisition of Alaska and of the Panama Territory.*

He severely embarrassed United States isthmian policy when he set up a slave republic in Nicaragua. The fault was not altogether Walker's. As he tries to explain in this document, written in an American jail shortly before he was released—only to be executed by an Honduran firing squad—the politics of slavery separated him from Northern backers of his original intention.

SOURCE. William Walker, *The War in Nicaragua* (Mobile, Alabama, 1860), pp. 257–280, *passim.*

The resulting tract, appealing for Southern support, represents the South's major contribution to Manifest Destiny ideology. The argument within it is by no means hypocritical, for Walker, a Tennessean by birth, had always leaned toward a swashbuckling cavalier tradition. Within this tradition, he was more philosophical and experimental than most, certainly among the most courageous persons who have ever lived by principle, in that he recognized the possibility of having to die for what might be only illusion of one's self-making. This self-awareness leads paradoxically to a seemingly very detached third-person narrative, the following selection from which is not typical. Though much has been written about Walker by historians, the best critical appreciation is Arthur D. Howden Smith's novel, A Manifest Destiny *(New York, 1926). This novel has the additional virtue of locating women in a picture of Manifest Destiny that is otherwise masculine. The only other concession to a woman's role is by way of Whitman's poem, "Passage to India," which pays respect to mothers of a supposedly superior American race. In Howden Smith's novel, women inspire every critical action, without whom men would not dare. No scholarly study has been made of women's role in Manifest Destiny.*

The men who framed the Constitution of the United States were not beyond the control of the influences which in France led to the horrors of Hayti and in England to the miseries of Jamaica. The wits and philosophers of the constitutional convention—the strong reason of Franklin and the brilliant genius of Hamilton, as well as the lofty soul of Washington—were not unaffected by the errors of the French reformers of the period. The mad rhapsodies of Rousseau, the sharp keen sarcasm of Voltaire, had infected the readers of that time with a sort of hydrophobia—a mortal aversion to the word *slavery*. Hamilton and Washington, though struggling against French notions, were still under the influence to some extent of the Genevese ravings about equality and fraternity. Mr. Jefferson not only yielded to the French fashions of thought and feeling, but actually cherished them as if they were the fruits of reason and philosophy. While such causes operated on the American leaders of the time, the people of the period were tainted with the notions of the English Buxton and Clarkson. The dissenters of Great Britain infused their opinions about the slave-trade into their religious brethren in America; and thus, by the union of French philosophy with English humanitarianism, the constitution of 1787 was burdened with clauses of which the evil effect is now constantly felt by the slaveholding communities of the United States.*

If the strong, broad minds of the constitutional convention of 1787 were not able to resist entirely the opinions prevalent in France and England concerning slavery, how much less were the poor, imitative creatures Spanish policy left to her American colonies after their independence able to withstand the prejudices of the European world. Spain had, in fact, left them with too little slavery to preserve their social order. Instead of maintaining the purity of the races as did the English in their settlements, the Spaniards had cursed their continental possessions with a mixed race. Hence it would have been little less than a miracle if the Spanish American States had at the moment of independence decided to retain slavery in their midst. It is only of late years that the really beneficial and conservative character of negro-slavery has begun to be appreciated in the United States.

For a long time it was the fashion, and with many it still is, to regard the Northern States of the Federal Union as the conservative element of American society. It is true that the Northern States are the conservative element of the federal government; because the Union is nearly altogether the creature of their will and of their interests. Therefore, on all occasions they have sought to strengthen the federal power through tariffs and banks and large schemes of internal improvement. But such conservatism as this does not touch the organic structure of society; it merely determines its external form and appearance. The conservatism of slavery is deeper than this; it goes to the vital relations of capital toward labor, and by the firm footing it gives the former it enables the intellect of society to push boldly forward in the pursuit of new forms of civilization. At present it is the struggle of free labor with slave labor which prevents the ener-

* For this paragraph the reader must review early national history, especially intellectual history.

gies of the former from being directed against the capital of the
North through the ingenious machinery of the ballot box and
universal suffrage; and it is difficult to conceive how capital can
be secured from the attacks of the majority in a pure democracy
unless with the aid of a force which gets its strength from slave
labor.

The Spanish American States, after their independence, aimed
to establish Republics without slavery; and the history of forty
years of disorder and public crime is fertile in lessons for him
who hath eyes to see and ears to hear. Carried away by his imagination, or rather by his sensibilities, Mr. Clay pleaded the cause
of Spanish American independence, and anticipated good government as the result of the movement. The policy he urged was
undobtedly wise both for the United States and for England,
inasmuch as it opened the old Spanish colonies to other commercial nations. But the effects of independence have not been beneficial on the people of the colonies themselves. Spain gave order, at least, to the possessions she held in the New World; and
order, attended as it was by exaction, sometimes even by extor-
tion, was better than the anarchy of so-called Republican rule. In
Nicaragua whole tracts which were cultivated under the Spanish
dominion have gone to waste since the independence; and the in-
digo of the Isthmus, which even ten years ago was a valuable article of export, has disappeared almost entirely from trade.

*If Spain, then, failed to leave her colonies with the internal
force or the system capable of re-organizing their independent
society, the plan immediately suggests itself of applying to them
the rules which have constructed a firm and harmonious civilization where the Anglo-American has found himself on the same
soil with one of the colored races.* The introduction of negro-
slavery into Nicaragua would furnish a supply of constant and
reliable labor requisite for the cultivation of tropical products.
With the negro-slave as his companion, the white man would become fixed to the soil; and they together would destroy the
power of the mixed race which is the bane of the country. The
pure Indian would readily fall into the new social organization;

*Italics are the present editor's. The major, premise of this passage is the
ruling one for the extracontinental phase of Manifest Destiny.

for he does not aim at political power, and only asks to be protected in the fruits of his industry. The Indian of Nicaragua, in
his fidelity and docility, as well as in his capacity for labor, approaches nearly the negroes of the United States; and he would
readily assume the manners and habits of the latter. In fact the
manners of the Indian toward the ruling race are now more sub-
missive than those of the American negro toward his
master. . . . The enemies of the only original form of American
civilization are many and powerful. They are resolute in their determination not merely to limit but to extirpate slavery. The man
who leads the free-labor myriads of the United States—he, whose
firm will and far-reaching mind do not quail either at the doctrines or the acts to which his political philosophy logically con-
ducts him, has already declared that he hopes to see the time
when the foot of not a slave shall press the continent. Yet the
sluggards of slavery say, "a little more rest, a little more folding
of the arms to slumber." Strafford sleeps though the axe of the
headsman is whetted for his execution.

*The contest between free and slave labor in the United States
not only touches the interests and destiny of those immediately
engaged in the struggle but it affects the fate of the whole continent. The question involved is whether the civilization of the
western world shall be European or American.** If free labor
prevails in its effort to banish slave labor from the continent, the
history of American society becomes a faint reflex of European
systems and prejudices, without contributing any new ideas, any
new sentiments, or any new institutions, to the mental and moral
wealth of the world. The necessary consequence of the triumph
of free labor will be the destruction, by a slow and cruel process,
of the colored races which now inhabit the central and southern
portions of the continent. The labor of the inferior races cannot
compete with that of the white race unless you give it a white
master to direct its energies; and without such protection as slavery affords, the colored races must inevitably succumb in the
struggle with white labor. Hence a Nicaraguan can not be an indifferent spectator of the contest between the two forms of labor
in the United States; and deeper yet must be his interest in the

* Italics are the present editor's.

matter if born and educated in a slave State of the Union, he re-
volves in his mind the results which will ensue to the home of
his childhood, and the firesides of the friends of his youth, in
case victory smiles upon the soldiers of free labor. Do not, therefore, men of the South, deem it the voice of a stranger, or of one
without a stake in your country's welfare, which urges you to
strike a blow in defence of your honor, no less than of your
hearths and your families, ere the blast of the enemy's bugle calls
upon you to surrender your arms to an overwhelming force.

The tongue of truth and friendship is not that of undue praise
or fawning flattery, and the soft songs of the suitor too often woo
to danger and destruction. Therefore, be not displeased, sons of
the South—for it is to you I now speak—if the criticism on your
acts and policy appear harsh or severe; but examine your conduct and that of your public servants for the last three years and
see whither it has led you. It is now but little more than three
years since you elected the President of your choice,* and in
your simplicity you thought this success a great victory. What
fruits have you reaped from it? Where are the rewards of your
campaign? In what triumphs of policy have all your toils and all
your efforts ended?

Your President—for he is the work of your hands—went into
office pledged to your policy in Kansas and in Central America.
He attempted to deceive you in Kansas, and your leaders drove
him to the course he was forced to pursue. Like sheep to the
slaughter he and his Northern friends were led to the support of
Southern policy in Kansas; but what has resulted from their sac-
rifice, or from all the efforts the Southern leaders made to drag
them to the altar? Was Kansas admitted into the Union? Did you
have even the empty pleasure of boasting over a barren victory?
The Kansas contest was made, as all admitted, for an abstract
right. Your leaders were true to you, because you were true to
yourselves, when contending for an "abstract right"; let us see
whether you and they were equally faithful to your honor and
your interests when contending for a right not abstract. . . . Is
it not time for the South to cease the contest for abstractions and

* This was President Buchanan, who proclaimed "popular Sovereignty" as
between slave and free territories.

to fight for realities? Of what avail is it to discuss the right to carry slaves into the territories of the Union, if there are none to go thither? These are questions for schoolmen—fit to sharpen the logical faculty and to make the mind quick and keen in the perception of analogies and distinctions; but surely they are not such questions as touch practical life and come home to men's interests and actions. The feelings and conscience of a people are not to be called forth by the subtleties of lawyers or the differences of metaphysicians; nor can their energies be roused into action for the defence of rights none of them care to exercise. The minds of full-grown men cannot be fed on mere discussions of territorial rights: they require some substantial policy which all can understand and appreciate.

Nor is it wise for the weaker party to waste its strength in fighting for shadows. It is only the stronger party which can afford to throw away its force on indecisive skirmishes. *At present the South must husband her political power else she will soon lose all she possesses. The same influence she brought to bear in favor of the position she took in Kansas would have secured the establishment of the Americans in Nicaragua.** And unless she assumes now an entirely defensive attitude, what else is left for the South except to carry out the policy proposed to her three years ago in Central America? How else can she strengthen slavery than by seeking its extension beyond the limits of the Union? The Republican party aims at destroying slavery by sap and not by assault. It declares now that the task of confining slavery is complete and the work of the miner has already commenced. Whither can the slaveholder fly when the enemy has completed his chambers and filled in the powder and prepared the train, and stands with lighted match ready to apply the fire?

Time presses. If the South wishes to get her institutions into tropical America she must do so before treaties are made to embarrass her action and hamper her energies. Already there is a treaty between Mexico and Great Britain by which the former agrees to do all in her power for the suppression of the slave-trade, and in 1856 a clause was inserted in the Dallas-Clarendon Convention, stipulating for the perpetual exclusion of slavery

* Italics are the present editor's.

from the Bay Islands of Honduras. This clause was suggested (as the writer was informed by the person himself who proposed it) by an American, for the purpose of securing the support of England to a projected railway across Honduras; and thus the rights of American civilization were to be bartered away for the paltry profits of a railroad company. And while Nicaragua was to be hemmed in by an anti-slavery treaty between England and Honduras on the north, Costa Rica made an agreement with New Granada that slavery should never be introduced within her limits. *The enemies of American civilization—for such are the enemies of slavery—seem to be more on the alert than its freinds.**

The faith which Walker had in the intelligence of the Southern States to perceive their true policy and in their resolution to carry it out, was one of the causes which led to the publication of the decree of the 22d of September at the time it was given forth. Nor is his faith in the South shaken; though who can fail to be amazed at the facility with which the South is carried off after chimeras? Sooner or later, however, the slaveholding States are bound to come as one man to the support of the Nicaraguan policy. *The decree of the 22d September, not the result of hasty passion or immature thought, fixed the fate of Nicaragua and bound the Republic to the car of American civilization.** For more than two years the enemies of slavery have been contriving and plotting to exclude the naturalized Nicaraguans from their adopted country. But as yet not a single additional barrier has been interposed; and the South has but to resolve upon the task of carrying slavery into Nicaragua in order that the work may be accomplished.

---

* Italics are the editor's. The railroad projector, Commodore Vanderbilt, successfully conspired with three "enemies" in bringing about Walker's undoing.

* Italics are the editor's. The statement is based on President Pierce's acceptance of an ambassador from this new slave republic under false pretexts not of Walker's own doing. Walker decreed Nicaragua a slave republic on September 22, 1856.

11   FROM   Orestes A. Brownson
     The Proper Name of the Country Is America

*This selection concludes the first phase of Manifest Destiny,
referring back to its New England colonial origins in the light of
the Civil War and from an American Catholic point of view
which accentuates the east-west thrust of American civilization
while it opposes imperialism. The major argument here is that
the whole North and South American hemisphere constitutes a
new West vis-à-vis old Europe. It lends an aggressive tone to the
Monroe Doctrine that was not present in its official form; yet, it
renounces any policy that would subjugate neighboring peoples.
Such a statement perhaps best illustrates what some historians
regard as an absence of ends and means within Manifest Destiny
ideology. Certainly it bears little relationship to the actual course
of invervention that President Theodore Roosevelt's administration later pursued in Latin America.*

*Orestes A. Brownson (1803–1876), social philosopher, au-
thor, and clergyman, devoted much of his life to the realization
of a social gospel, a cause that took him from Protestant pulpits
to the streets, where he helped form the short-lived Working-
men's party. As a convert to Catholicism in 1844, he tried to lib-
eralize the church's social policies.*

The Jews were the chosen people of God, through whom the
primitive traditions were to be preserved in their purity and integrity, and the Messiah was to come. The Greeks were the chosen people of God, for the development and realization of the
beautiful or the divine splendor in art, and of the true in science
and philosophy; and the Romans, for the development of the
state, law, and jurisprudence. The great despotic nations of Asia

SOURCE. Orestes A. Brownson, *The American Republic* (New York, 1865),
pp. 4–5, 392–393, 435–437, 439.

were never properly nations; or if they were nations with a mission, they proved false to it, and count for nothing in the progressive development of the human race. History has not recorded their mission, and as far as they are known they have contributed only to the abnormal development or corruption of religion and civilization. Despotism is barbaric and abnormal.

The United States, or the American Republic, has a mission, and is chosen of God for the realization of a great idea. It has been chosen not only to continue the work assigned to Greece and Rome, but to accomplish a greater work than was assigned to either. In art, it will prove false to its mission if it do not rival Greece; and in science and philosophy, if it do not surpass it. In the state, in law, in jurisprudence, it must continue and surpass Rome. Its idea is liberty, indeed, but liberty with law, and law with liberty. Yet its mission is not so much the realization of liberty as the realization of the true idea of the state, which secures at once the authority of the public and the freedom of the individual—the sovereignty of the people without social despotism, and individual freedom without anarchy. In other words, its mission is to bring out in its life the dialectic union of authority and liberty, of the natural rights of man and those of society. . . .

Of all the states or colonies on this continent, the American Republic alone has a destiny, or the ability to add any thing to the civilization of the race. Canada and the other British Provinces, Mexico and Central America, Columbia and Brazil, and the rest of the South American States, might be absorbed in the United States without being missed by the civilized world. They represent no idea, and the work of civilization could go on without them as well as with them. If they keep up with the progress of civilization, it is all that can be expected of them. France, England, Germany, and Italy might absorb the rest of Europe, and all Asia and Africa, without withdrawing a single laborer from the work of advancing the civilization of the race; and it is doubtful if these nations themselves can severally or jointly advance it much beyond the point reached by the Roman Empire, except in abolishing slavery and including in the political people the whole territorial people. They can only develop and give a general application to the fundamental principles of the Roman constitution. That indeed is much, but it adds no new element nor new combination of pre-existing elements. But nothing of this can be said of the United States. . . .

Count de Maistre predicted early in the century the failure of the United States, because they have no proper name; but his prediction assumed what is not the fact. The United States have a proper name by which all the world knows and calls them. The proper name of the country is America: that of the people is Americans. Speak of Americans simply, and nobody understands you to mean the people of Canada, Mexico, Brazil, Peru, Chile, Paraguay, but everybody understands you to mean the people of the United States. The fact is significant, and foretells for the people of the United States a continental destiny, as is also foreshadowed in the so-called "Monroe doctrine," which France, during our domestic troubles, was permitted, on condition of not intervening in our civil war in favor of the rebellion, to violate.

There was no statesmanship in proclaiming the "Monroe doctrine," for the statesman keeps always, as far as possible, his government free to act according to the exigencies of the case when it comes up, unembarrassed by previous declarations of principles. Yet the doctrine only expresses the destiny of the American people, and which nothing but their own fault can prevent them from realizing in its own good time. Napoleon will not succeed in his Mexican policy, and Mexico will add some fifteen or twenty new States to the American Union as soon as it is clearly for the interests of all parties that it should be done, and it can be done by mutual consent, without war or violence. The Union will fight to maintain the integrity of her domain and the supremacy of her laws within it, but she can never, consistently with her principles or her interests, enter upon a career of war and conquest. Her system is violated, endangered, not extended, by subjugating her neighbors, for subjugation and liberty go not together. Annexation, when it takes place, must be on terms of perfect equality, and by the free act of the state annexed. The Union can admit of no inequality of rights and franchises between the States of which it is composed. The Canadian Provinces and the Mexican and Central American States, when annexed, must be as free as the original States of the Union, sharing alike in the power and the protection of the Republic—alike in its authority, its freedom, its grandeur, and its glory, as one free, independent, self-governing people. They may gain much, but must lose nothing by annexation. . . . The American people need not trouble themselves about their exterior expansion. That will come of itself as fast as desirable.

12 FROM   *Herman Melville*
                      Allons, Vivenza!

This passage, which can be read as a kind of epilogue to the period, combines the gusto of Whitman in his poem "Passage to India" with Melville's propensity for metaphysical doubts. These doubts account for reading difficulty in getting into the passage, as they are advanced by a medley of voices unanchored in conventional time and place. The novel from which this passage is taken advances rapidly from realistic adventure, on the order of Typee, *to wild flights of allegorical imagination. In this allegory, the Pacific island of Vivenza represents the United States, Dominora is England, King Media is the voice of conventional reason, Babbalanja is a garrulous, eclectic philosopher, and Porpheero are the lands beyond the Philippines. No speaker in this passage will take responsibility for the anonymous scroll that introduces it. The only other memorable allegory at the expense of Manifest Destiny is Hawthorne's tale of "The Celestial Railroad," which assails the idea of progress through technology more than it fulminates against Manifest Destiny.*

[The Scroll begins:] "But, as in stars you have written it on the welkin, sovereign kings! you are a great and glorious people. And verily, yours is the best and happiest land under the sun. But not wholly, because you, in your wisdom, decreed it: your

SOURCE. An authoritative reprint of the original 1849 edition of *Mardi and a Voyage Thither* by Russell and Russell, Inc., 2 volumes (New York, 1963), *II*, pp. 243–270, *passim*.

origin and geography necessitated it. Nor, in their germ, are all your blessings to be ascribed to the noble sires, who of yore fought in your behalf, sovereign kings! Your nation enjoyed no little independence before your declaration declared it. Your ancient pilgrims fathered your liberty; and your wild woods harboured the nursling. For the state that to-day is made up of slaves, cannot to-morrow transmute her bond into free; though lawlessness may transform them into brutes. Freedom is the name for a thing that is *not* freedom; this, a lesson never learned in an hour or an age. By some tribes it will never be learned. . . .

"Students of history are horror-struck at the massacres of old; but in the shambles men are being murdered to-day. Could time be reversed, and the future change places with the past, the past would cry out against us, and our future, full as loudly as we against the ages foregone. All the Ages are his children, calling each other names.

"Hark ye, sovereign kings! cheer not on the yelping pack too furiously. Hunters have been torn by their hounds. Be advised; wash your hands. Hold aloof. Oro has poured out an ocean for an everlasting barrier between you and the worst folly which other republics have perpetrated. That barrier hold sacred. And swear never to cross over to Porpheero, by manifesto or army, unless you traverse dry land.

"And be not too grasping, nearer home. It is not freedom to filch. Expand not your area too widely, now. Seek you proselytes? Neighbouring nations may be free, without coming under your banner. And if you cannot lay your ambition, know this: that it is best served by waiting events.

"Time, but Time only, may enable you to cross the equator; and give you the Arctic Circles for your boundaries."

So read the anonymous scroll; which straightway was torn into shreds. . . .

Once more embarking, we gained Vivenza's south-western side; and there beheld vast swarms of labourers discharging from canoes great loads of earth; which they tossed upon the beach.

"It is true, then," said Media, "that these freemen are engaged in digging down other lands, and adding them to their own, piece-meal. And this, they call extending their dominions agriculturally, and peaceably."

"My lord, they pay a price for every canoe load," said Mohi.

"Ay, old man, holding the spear in one hand, and striking the bargain with the other."

"Yet charge it not upon all Vivenza," said Babbalanja. "Some of her tribes are hostile to these things: and when their countrymen fight for land, are only warlike in opposing war."

"And therein, Babbalanja, is involved one of those anomalies in the condition of Vivenza," said Media, "which I can hardly comprehend. How comes it, that with so many things to divide them, the valley-tribes still keep their mystic league intact?"

"All plain, it is because the model, when they derive their union, is one of nature's planning. My lord, have you ever observed the mysterious federation subsisting among the mollusca of the Tunicata order,—in other words, a species of cuttle-fish, abounding at the bottom of the lagoon?"

"Yes: in clear weather about the reefs, I have beheld them time and again: but never with an eye to their political condition."

"Ah! my lord king, we should not cut off the nervous communication between our eyes and our cerebellums."

"What were you about to say concerning the Tunicata order of mollusca, sir philosopher?"

"My very honourable lord, I hurry to conclude. They live in a compound structure; but though connected by membranous canals, freely communicating throughout the league—each member has a heart and stomach of its own; provides and digests its own dinners; and grins and bears its own gripes, without imparting the same to its neighbours. But if a prowling shark touches one member, it ruffles all. Precisely thus now with Vivenza. In that confederacy, there are as many consciences as tribes; hence, if one member on its own behalf assumes aught afterward repudiated, the sin rests on itself alone; is not participated." . . .

West, West! West, West! Whitherward point Hope and prophet-fingers; whitherward, at sunset, kneel all worshippers of fire; whitherward in mid-ocean, the great whales turn to die; whitherward face all the Moslem dead in Persia; whitherward lie

Heaven and Hell!—West, West! Whitherward mankind and empires—flocks, caravans, armies, navies; worlds, suns, and stars all wend!—West, West!—Oh boundless boundary! Eternal goal! Whitherward rush, in thousand worlds, ten thousand thousand keels! Beacon, by which the universe is steered!—Like the north star, attracting all needles! Unattainable forever; but forever leading to great things this side thyself!—Hive of all sunsets!—Gabriel's pinions may not overtake thee!

PART THREE

The Indian Question

QUOTABLE QUOTES

"The utmost good faith shall always be observed towards the Indians; their land and property shall never be taken from them without their consent; and in their property, rights and liberty, they shall never be invaded or disturbed, unless in justified and lawful wars authorized by Congress; but laws founded in justice and humanity shall from time to time be made, for preventing wrongs being done to them, and for preserving peace and friendship with them."

from The Northwest Ordinance, 1787

"Colorado is as greedy and unjust in 1880 as was Georgia in 1830, and Ohio in 1795; and the United States Government breaks promises now as deftly as then, and with an added ingenuity from long experience. One of its strongest supports in so doing is the wide-spread sentiment among the people of dislike to the Indian, of impatience with his presence as a 'barrier to civilization,' and distrust of it as a possible danger. The old tales of the frontier life, with its horrors of Indian warfare, have gradually, by two or three generations' telling, produced in the average mind something like an hereditary instinct of unquestioning and unreasoning aversion which it is almost impossible to dislodge or soften. There are hundreds of pages of unimpeachable testimony on the side of the Indian; but it goes for nothing, is set down as sentimentalism or partisanship, tossed aside and forgotten."

Helen Hunt Jackson, 1881

"The rich and beautiful valleys of Wyoming are destined for the occupancy and sustenance of the Anglo-Saxon race. The wealth that for untold ages has lain hidden beneath the snow-capped summits of our mountains has been placed there by Providence to reward the brave spirits whose lot it is to compose the advance-guard of civilization. The Indians must stand aside or be overwhelmed by the ever advancing and ever increasing tide of emigration. The destiny of the aborigines is written in characters not to be mistaken. The same inscrutable Arbiter that decreed the downfall of Rome has pronounced the doom of extinction upon the red men of America."

Cheyenne Daily Leader, March 3, 1870

"It was wholly impossible to avoid conflicts with the weaker race, unless we were willing to see the American continent fall into the hands of some other strong power; and even had we adopted such a ludicrous policy, the Indians themselves would have made war upon us. It cannot be too often insisted that they did not own the land; or, at least, that their ownership was merely such as that claimed often by our own white hunters. If the Indians really owned Kentucky in 1775, then in 1776 it was the property of Boon and his associates; and to dispossess one party was as great a wrong as to dispossess the other."

Theodore Roosevelt, 1889

13 FROM   *John Pendleton Kennedy and William Wirt Remember the Cherokee Nation*

The fate of the Cherokees, the largest and most culturally advanced of the Southeastern Indian tribes, comparable in importance to the Iroquois Confederacy in the Northeast, perhaps typifies American-Indian relations during the United States westward expansion. It provides an important test case with respect to the charges of imperialism that were leveled against Manifest Destiny. Presumably secured forever in their possessions and jurisdiction within the state of Georgia by federal authority, the Cherokees—the bulk of them at least, numbering approximately 20,000 people—were forcibly removed to the Indian Territory across the Mississippi in 1838 after a period of litigation that resulted from the pressure of whites to obtain their lands. Earlier, President Jefferson had thought of the trans-Mississippi West as a permanent, inviolable Indian preserve. In 1830, partly as a result of the Cherokee controversy, Congress passed a general Indian Removal Act securing Indians in their new homes under treaties to be transacted when a need arose. Such a treaty was extracted from a Cherokee minority and was by degrees eroded

SOURCE. John P. Kennedy, *Memoirs of the Life of William Wirt*, 2 vols. (Philadelphia, 1856) , *II*, pp. 294–297.

after the Civil War as white settlers infiltrated the Indian Territory. In 1892, the western "Cherokee Strip" was sold, and in 1906 the tribe was disbanded.

William Wirt (1772–1834), a prominent Virginian author, lawyer, and United States Attorney General under Presidents Monroe and John Quincy Adams, defended the Cherokees before the United States Supreme Court, opposing the strong will of President Andrew Jackson, while knowing that his countrymen would consider him a pariah. This selection begins with his summary address to the Supreme Court. His phrase, "Remember the Cherokee Nation," recalls other phrases that commemorate a time of national infamy such as "Remember the Maine" and "Remember Pearl Harbor." But Southern novelist, John Pendleton Kennedy (1795–1870), in the following gloss on Wirt's address, manages to take the sting out of Wirt's impassioned plea. Chief Justice John Marshall's reluctant refusal to take jurisdiction in the case, quite aside from considerations of a popular will in the matter, hinged mainly on the question of whether the Cherokees constituted an independent, sovereign nation within the state of Georgia. If the answer had been clearly yes, Marshall's Court would have established a strong legal precedent for reading imperialism into United States continental expansion along the classic imperialistic lines. Although the Cherokees were more clearly a separate nation than most Indian tribes, with a constitution, a settled mode of life, and even a written language, the legal ambiguity was never resolved, and Indians were variously treated in law as limited sovereign nations, as "wards" of the United States akin to welfare recipients, as colonial subjects, and as individuals with second-class citizenship.

In the very next year (1832), a judge of the Alabama Supreme Court in the case of Caldwell vs. The State of Alabama resorted to the language of imperialism in that state's verdict against the Creeks: "The effect of acquisition by conquest is to vest all the national rights of the conquered, in the conqueror, and because all right to the soil among Indian tribes was national, none individual, the right of soil, as well as sovereignty, passed to the conqueror." So naked an expression of imperialism, understandably, never found its way into authoritative

American law. The strongest moral case for American imperial-
ism vis-à-vis the Indians is presented by Helen Hunt Jackson in
her muckraking A Century of Dishonor *(New York, 1881),*
which concludes with the example of the Cherokee nation. She is
represented very well here in a head-note quotation that intro-
duces this section. A definitive answer to such criticism is that of
Theodore Roosevelt, which concludes this section.

"I have presented to you all the views that have occurred to
me as bearing materially on this question. I have endeavoured to
satisfy you that, according to the supreme law of the land, you
have before you proper parties and a proper case to found your
original jurisdiction: that the case is one which warrants and
most imperiously demands an injunction; and unless its aspect be
altered by an answer and evidence—which I confidently believe
it cannot be—that if ever there was a case which called for a decree of perpetual peace, this is the case.

"It is with no ordinary feelings that I am about to take leave
of this cause. The existence of this remnant of a once great and
mighty nation is at stake; and it is for your honours to say
whether they shall be blotted out from the creation, in utter disregard of all our treaties. They are here in the last extremity, and
with them must perish forever the honour of the American
name. The faith of our nation is fatally linked with their existence, and the blow which destroys them quenches forever our
own glory: for what glory can there be, of which a patriot can be
proud, after the good name of his country shall have departed?
We may gather laurels on the field and trophies on the ocean,
but they will never hide this foul blot upon our escutcheon. 'Remember the Cherokee Nation'—will be answer enough to the
proudest boasts that we can ever make; answer enough to cover
with confusion the face and the heart of every man among us, in
whose bosom the last spark of grace has not been extinguished.
Such, it is possible, there may be who are willing to glory in their
own shame, and to triumph in the disgrace which they are permitted to heap upon this nation. But, thank Heaven! they are

comparatively few. The great majority of the American people see this subject in its true light. They have hearts of flesh in their bosoms, instead of hearts of stone; and every rising and setting sun witnesses the smoke of the incense from the thousands and tens of thousands of domestic altars, ascending to the throne of grace to invoke its guidance and blessing on your councils. The most undoubting confidence is reposed in this tribunal.

"We know that whatever can be properly done for this unfortunate people will be done by this honourable court. This cause is one that must come to every honest and feeling heart. They have been true and faithful to us, and have a right to expect a corresponding fidelity on our part. Through a long course of years, they have followed our counsel with the docility of children. Our wish has been their law. We asked them to become civilized, and they became so. They assumed our dress, copied our names, pursued our course of education, adopted our form of government, embraced our religion, and have been proud to imitate us in every thing in their power. They have watched the progress of our prosperity with the strongest interest, and have marked the rising grandeur of our nation with as much interest as if they had belonged to us. They have even adopted our resentments, and in our war with the Seminole tribes, they voluntarily joined our arms, and gave effectual aid in driving back those barbarians from the very State that now oppresses them. They threw upon the field in that war, a body of men who proved, by their martial bearing, their descent from the noble race that were once the lords of these extensive forests; men worthy to associate with the 'lion,' who, in their own language, 'walks upon the mountain-tops.' They fought side by side with our present Chief Magistrate, and received his repeated thanks for their gallantry and conduct.

"May it please your honours, they have refused to us no gratification which it has been in their power to grant. We asked them for a portion of their lands, and they ceded it. We asked again and again, and they continued to cede, until they have now reduced themselves within the narrowest compass that their own subsistence will permit. What return are we about to make to them for all this kindness? We have pledged for their protection, and for the guarantee of the remainder of their lands, the faith and honour of the nation; a faith and honour never sullied, nor even drawn into question till now. We promised them, and they trusted us. They have trusted us: shall they be deceived? They would as soon expect to see their rivers run upwards on their sources, or the sun roll back in his career, as that the United States would prove false to them, and false to the word so solemnly pledged by their Washington, and renewed and perpetuated by his illustrious successors.

"Is this the high mark to which the American nation has been so strenuously and successfully pressing forward? Shall we sell the mighty meed of our high honours at so worthless a price, and, in two short years, cancel all the glory which we have been gaining before the world for the last half century? Forbid it, Heaven!

"I will hope for better things. There is a spirit that will yet save us. I trust that we shall find it here, in this sacred court, where no foul and malignant demon of party enters to darken the understanding or to deaden the heart, but where all is clear, calm, pure, vital and firm. I cannot believe that this honourable court, possessing the power of preservation, will stand by and see these people stripped of their property and extirpated from the earth, while they are holding up to us their treaties and claiming the fulfilment of our engagements. If truth and faith and honour and justice have fled from every other part of our country, we shall find them here. If not, our sun has gone down in treachery, blood and crime, in the face of the world; and, instead of being proud of our country, as heretofore, we may well call upon the rocks and mountains to hide our shame from earth and heaven."

The fate of this application is well known.* The court decided the preliminary question,—that of the jurisdiction,—against the complainants. The opinion was carefully prepared by Chief Justice Marshall, and was delivered manifestly with regret. "If courts were permitted," said he, "to indulge their sympathies, a case better calculated to excite them can scarcely be imagined. A people, once numerous, powerful and truly independent, found by our ancestors in the quiet and uncontrolled possession of an ample domain, gradually sinking beneath our superior policy,

* Kennedy's commentary begins here.

our arts and our arms, have yielded their lands by successive treaties, each of which contains a solemn guarantee of the residue, until they retain no more of their formerly extensive territory than is deemed necessary to their comfortable subsistence. To preserve this remnant, the present application is made." The question of jurisdiction was one upon which Mr. Wirt, from the first, entertained doubts; but his opinion in favour of it was confirmed by the high authority of Chancellor Kent and other eminent lawyers. The Chancellor's opinion was read in the discussion of the case; it was carefully studied and strongly pronounced. In the Court, the decision was not unanimous:—Judges Thompson and Story dissented. But, amidst these conflicts of opinion, the Cherokees were defeated.

Few persons, at the present day, will lament this defeat. It opened to the tribe a better destiny. The fervour of the orator is but an imperfect gauge of the wisdom of the statesman. For the sake of the instruction it imparts, it is often worth the labour to compare the glowing prophecies which are uttered in the inspiration of a heated fancy with the subsequent revelations of time. Mr. Wirt's impassioned peroration, which we have just read, affords an example that may be studied. Neither have the Cherokees been "blotted out from creation," nor has "the honour of the American name" forever perished. I have before me the last report of the Indian agent, upon the condition of the Cherokees, in their home beyond the Mississippi—the report of 1848. "The Cherokees," he informs the Government, "are in a prosperous condition, so far as agricultural pursuits are concerned. Many of them have large and extensive farms, under good fences and well cultivated. Peace and order prevailed (in their council at Tahlaquah, the seat of government) to an extent not very common in legislative bodies, and I hesitate not to say that, if the different parties were again united so as to confide in each other, they are as capable of managing their own affairs, in a territorial or state government, as most people are in a territorial or new state government.

"With regard to the females, they are generally industrious and very neat in their household affairs. You generally find them neatly and fashionably dressed in home-made clothes of their own manufacturing. In passing through the country, the wheel and the loom are frequently the first sounds that greet your ear.

"With regard to the progress of religion and literature in the Cherokee Nation, I am advised that I may readily set it down, that, in each, there has been at least an improvement of ten per cent. from the last nine years' report. The two seminaries are in progress of building. The following branches of education have been taught:—spelling, reading, writing, arithmetic, geography, grammar, natural and mental philosophy, algebra and composition. Many of the scholars made good progress in their studies, and, at the public examination, acquitted themselves much to their own credit and the satisfaction of a large number of spectators, comprising some of the leading men of the nation, among whom was the acting principal chief and one or two members of the legislature."

This is a promising picture, and may somewhat reconcile us to the wrongs of which we have given the history.*

* This judgment does not square with historical fact since 1856, when Kennedy published this *Memoir*.

14 FROM *Diverse American Indians*
I Have Spoken

And indeed they did, most eloquently and to little avail. A few spoke in English, most spoke in their native tongues; and many had derogatory statements to make about the white man's use of the printed word, which signified to them broken treaties and a misuse of technological magic in the interest of greed. No major historian of Manifest Destiny has seemed to consider their first-hand testimonies relevant. Remarkably, a recent collection of documents entitled The Indian and the White Man, *edited by*

SOURCE. (1) Creek Chief Speckled Snake, 1829, *Niles' Weekly Register*, XXXVI, No. 36 (June 20, 1829), 274. (2) Washington Territory Chief Seattle, 1854, in Archie Binns, *Northwest Gateway.* . . (New York, 1941), pp. 100–104. (3) Sioux Chief Red Cloud, 1870, as reported in the *New York Times* for June 17, 1870. (4) Shaman Black Elk of the Dakota Sioux, 1912, in John G. Neihardt, *Black Elk Speaks* (New York, 1932), pp. 219–220. (5) Anaquoness, Ojibway, 1918, in Wa-Sha-Quon-Asin, *Tales of an Empty Cabin* (New York, 1936), pp. 91–95.

Wilcomb E. Washburn (New York University press, 1964), includes only two authentic Indian testimonies among 112 entries! My own sources draw heavily on Virginia Irving Armstrong, editor, I Have Spoken: American History Through the Voices of the Indians (Chicago, 1971). The following excerpts proceed in chronological order, from 1829 to 1918, the last of which alone is written (in English) rather than spoken. The rest are believed to be rather faithful translations.

The last testimony, that of Anaquoness, Ojibway, to his World War I nurse, is included because it conveys in very personal terms the great difference between an abstract, metaphysical view of natural environment, such as characterized Manifest Destiny, and a true reverence for the same environment. It further serves to point up the ironies of a supposedly superior civilization which proliferates luxuries that do not delight, supports religions that do not console, boasts political institutions that do not represent, and protects conglomerate business enterprises that cannot serve the poor or respect the natural environment— while an American under-class, more numerous by millions than the Indian population, still has to contend with starvation and disease. A further irony, which has played into the hands of Manifest Destiny ideologues, is that three fifths of the rest of the world yet hankers for this kind of civilization. If this later expansion of American influence be imperialism, it has taken a strange form that defies classical definition. An authoritative Indian view of Manifest Destiny is Dee Brown's Bury My Heart at Wounded Knee: An Indian History of the American West *(New York: Holt, Rinehart and Winston, 1970). The legalistic rationale for retiring Indian claims to the American continent is examined by Vine Deloria, Jr., editor,* Of Utmost Faith *(San Francisco: Straight Arrow Books, 1971).*

1.

Brothers: We have heard the talk of our Great Father; it is very kind. He says he loves his red children. . . .

When the first white man came over the wide waters, he was

but a little man . . . very little. His legs were cramped by sitting long in his big boat, and he begged for a little land. . . .

When he came to these shores the Indians gave him land, and kindled fires to make him comfortable. . . .

But when the white man had warmed himself at the Indian's fire, and had filled himself with the Indian's hominy, he became very large. He stopped not at the mountain tops, and his foot covered the plains and the valleys. His hands grasped the eastern and western seas. Then he became our Great Father. He loved his red children, but he said: "You must move a little farther, lest by accident I tread on you."

With one foot he pushed the red men across the Oconee, and with the other he trampled down the graves of our fathers. . . .

On another occasion he said, "Get a little farther; go beyond the Oconee and the Ocmulgee [Indian settlements in South Carolina and Georgia]—there is a pleasant country." He also said, "It shall be yours forever."

Now he says, "The land you live upon is not yours. Go beyond the Mississippi; there is game; there you may remain while the grass grows and the rivers run."

Will not our Great Father come there also? He loves his red children, and his tongue is not forked.

Brothers! I have listened to a great many talks from our Great Father. But they always began and ended in this—"Get a little farther; you are too near me." I have spoken.

2.

Yonder sky that has wept tears of compassion upon my people for centuries untold, and which to us appears changeless and eternal, may change. Today is fair. Tomorrow it may be overcast with clouds. My words are like the stars that never change. Whatever Seattle says the great chief at Washington can rely upon with as much certainty as he can upon the return of the sun or the seasons. The White Chief says that Big Chief at Washington sends us greetings of friendship and goodwill. That is kind of him for we know he has little need of our friendship in return. His people are many. They are like the grass that covers vast prairies. My people are few. They resemble the scattering trees of a storm-swept plain . . . I will not dwell on, nor mourn over, our untimely decay, nor reproach our paleface brothers with hastening it, as we too may have been somewhat to blame. . . .

Your God is not our God. Your God loves your people and hates mine. He folds his strong and protecting arms lovingly about the paleface and leads him by the hand as a father leads his infant son—but He has forsaken His red children—if they really are his. Our God, the Great Spirit, seems also to have forsaken us. Your God makes your people strong every day. Soon they will fill the land. Our people are ebbing away like a rapidly receding tide that will never return. The white man's God cannot love our people or He would protect them. They seem to be orphans who can look nowhere for help. How then can we be brothers? . . . We are two distinct races with separate origins and separate destinies. There is little in common between us.

To us the ashes of our ancestors are sacred and their resting place is hallowed ground. You wander far from the graves of your ancestors and seemingly without regret. Your religion was written upon tables of stone by the iron finger of your God so that you could not forget. The Red Man could never comprehend nor remember it. Our religion is the traditions of our ancestors—the dreams of our old men, given them in solemn hours of night by the Great Spirit; and the visions of our sachems; and it is written in the hearts of our people.

Your dead cease to love you and the land of their nativity as soon as they pass the portals of the tomb and wander way beyond the stars. They are soon forgotten and never return. Our dead never forget the beautiful world that gave them being.

Day and night cannot dwell together. The Red Man has ever fled the approach of the White Man, as the morning mist flees before the morning sun. However, your proposition seems fair and I think that my people will accept it and will retire to the reservation you offer them. Then we will dwell apart in peace. . . . It matters little where we pass the remnant of our days. They will not be many. A few more moons; a few more winters—and not one of the descendants of the mighty hosts that once moved over this broad land or lived in happy homes, protected by the Great Spirit, will remain to mourn over the graves of a people once more powerful and hopeful than yours. But why should I mourn at the untimely fate of my people? Tribe follows tribe, and nation follows nation, like the waves of the sea. It is the order of nature, and regret is useless. Your time of decay may be distant, but it will surely come, for even the White Man whose God walked and talked with him as friend with friend, cannot be exempt from the common destiny. We may be brothers after all. We will see. . . .

Every part of this soil is sacred in the estimation of my people. Every hillside, every valley, every plain and grove, has been hallowed by some sad or happy event in days long vanished. The very dust upon which you now stand responds more lovingly to their footsteps than to yours, because it is rich with the blood of our ancestors and our bare feet are conscious of the sympathetic touch. Even the little children who lived here and rejoiced here for a brief season will love these somber solitudes and at eventide they greet shadowy returning spirits. And when the last Red Man shall have perished, and the memory of my tribe shall have become a myth among the White Men, these shores will swarm with the invisible dead of my tribe, and when your children's children think themselves alone in the field, the store, the shop, upon the highway, or in the silence of the pathless woods, they will not be alone. At night when the streets of your cities and villages are silent and you think them deserted, they will throng with the returning hosts that once filled and still love this beautiful land. The White Man will never be alone.

Let him be just and deal kindly wtih my people, for the dead are not powerless. Dead, did I say? There is no death, only a change of worlds.

3.

My Brothers and my Friends who are before me today: God Almighty has made us all, and He is here to hear what I have to say to you today. The Great Spirit made us both. He gave me lands and He gave you lands. You came here and we received you as brothers. When the Almighty made you, He made you all white and clothed you. When He made us He made us with red skins and poor. When you first came we were very many and you were few. Now you are many and we are few. You do not know who appears before you to speak. He is a representative of the original American race, and first people of this continent. We are good, and not bad. The reports which you get about us are all on one side. You hear of us only as murderers and thieves. We are not so. If we had more lands to give to you we would give them, but we have no more. We are driven into a very little island, and we want you, our dear friends, to help us with the Government of the United States. The Great Spirits made us poor and ignorant. He made you rich and wise and skillful in things which we know nothing about. The good Father made you to eat tame game and us to eat wild game. Ask any one who has gone through to California. They will tell you we have treated them well. You have children. We, too, have children, and we wish to bring them up well. We ask you to help us do it. At the mouth of Horse Creek, in 1852, the Great Father made a treaty with us. We agreed to let him pass through our territory unharmed for fifty-five years. We kept our word. We committed no murders, no depredations, until the troops came there. When the troops were sent there trouble and disturbance arose. Since that time there have been various goods sent from time to time to us, but only once did they reach us, and soon the Great Father took away the only good man he had sent us, Col. Fitzpatrick. The Great Father said we must go to farming, and some of our men went to farming near Fort Laramie, and were treated very badly indeed. We came to Washington to see our Great Father that peace might be continued. The Great Father that made us both wishes peace to be kept; we want to keep peace. Will you help us? In 1868 men came out and brought papers. We could not read them, and they did not tell us truly what was in them. We thought the treaty was to remove the forts and that we should then cease from fighting. But they wanted to send us traders on the Missouri. We did not want to go on the Missouri, but wanted traders where we were. When I reached Washington the Great Father explained to me what the treaty was, and showed me that the interpreters had deceived me. All I want is right and justice. I have tried to get from the Great Father what is right and just. I have not altogether succeeded. I want you to help me to get what is right and just. I represent the whole Sioux nation, and they will be bound by what I say. I am no Spotted Tail, to say one thing one day and be bought for a pin the next. Look at me. I am poor and naked, but I am the Chief of the nation. We do not want riches, but we want to train our children right. Riches would do us no good. We could not take them with us to the other world. We do not want riches, we want peace and love.

The riches that we have in this world, Secretary [of the Interior Jacob] Cox said truly, we cannot take with us to the next world. Then I wish to know why Commissioners are sent out to us who do nothing but rob us and get the riches of this world away from us! I was brought up among the traders, and those who came out there in the early times treated me well and I had a good time with them. They taught us to wear clothes and to use tobacco and ammunition. But, by and by, the Great Father sent out a different kind of men; men who cheated and drank whisky; men who were so bad that the Great Father could not keep them at home and so sent them out there. I have sent a great many words to the Great Father but they never reached him. They were drowned on the way, and I was afraid the words I spoke lately to the Great Father would not reach you, so I came to speak to you myself; and now I am going away to my home. I want to have men sent out to my people whom we know and can trust. I am glad I have come here. You belong in the East and I belong in the West, and I am glad I have come here and that we could understand one another. I am very much obliged to you for listening to me. I go home this afternoon. I hope you will think of what I have said to you. I bid you all an affectionate farewell.

4.

Hey-a-a-hey!   Hey-a-a-hey!   Hey-a-a-hey!   Hey-a-ahey! Grandfather, Great Spirit, once more behold me on earth and lean to hear my feeble voice. You lived first, and you are older than all need, older than all prayer. All things belong to you— the two-legged, the four-legged, the wings of the air and all green things that live. You have set the powers of the four quarters of the earth to cross each other. The good road and the road of difficulties you have made me cross; and where they cross, the place is holy. Day in, day out, forevermore, you are the life of things.

Therefore I am sending you a voice, Great Spirit, my Grandfather, foregetting nothing you have made, the stars of the universe and the grasses of the earth.

You have said to me when I was still young and could hope,

that in difficulty I could send a voice four times, once for each quarter of the earth, and you would hear me.

Today I send a voice for a people in despair.

You have given me a sacred pipe, and through this I should make my offering. You see it now!

From the west you have given me the cup of living water and the sacred bow, the power to make life and to destroy it. You have given me the sacred wind and the herb from where the white giant lives—the cleansing power and the healing. The daybreak star and the pipe, you have given me from the east; and from the south the nation's sacred hoop and the tree that was to bloom. To the center of the world you have taken me and showed the goodness and the beauty and the strangeness of the greening earth, the only mother, and there the spirit-shapes of things, as they should be, you have shown me, and I have seen. At the center of the sacred hoop you have said that I should make the tree to bloom.

With tears running, O Great Spirit, my Grandfather—with running eyes I must say now that the tree has never bloomed. A pitiful old man, you see me here, and I have fallen away and done nothing. Here at the center of the world, where you took me when I was young and taught me; here, old I stand, and the tree is withered, my Grandfather.

Again, and maybe the last time on earth, I recall the great vision you sent me. It may be that some little root of the sacred tree still lives. Nourish it, then, that it may leaf and bloom and fill with singing birds. Hear me, not for myself but for my people; I am old. Hear me, that they may once more go back into the sacred hoop and find the good road and the shielding tree.

5.

February 3, 1918

Dear Miss Nurse:

Nearly four months now the Canada geese flew south and the snow is very deep. . . . The wee sorryful animals I tol you about sit around me tonight. . . . I seen my old old trees and the rocks that I know and the forest that is to me what your house is to you. . . . I wisht youd ben here to see when I got back. The In-

juns were camped and had their tents at the Head of the lake. I
went up. They come out and looked at me and the chief took me
by the hand and said How, and they all come one at a time and
shake hands and say How. They ast me nothin about the War
but said they would dance the Morning Wind dance, as I just
come from the East and that is the early morning wind on the
lakes. Then they dance the next night the Neebiche, meanin the
leaves that are blown and drift before the wind in the empty
forest. . . . Gee I'm lucky to travel the big woods agen. To us
peple the woods and the big hills and the Northen lights and the
sunsets are all alive and we live with these things and live in the
spirit of the woods like no white person can do. The big lakes we
travel on, the little lonely lakes we set our beaver traps on with a
ring of big black pines standin in rows lookin always north, like
they were watchin for somethin that never comes, same as the
Injun, they are real to us and when we are alone we speak to
them and are not lonesome. only thinkin always of the long ago
days and the old men. So we live in the past and the rest of the
world keeps goin by. For all their modern inventions they cant
live the way we do and they die if they try becase they cant read
the sunset and hear the old men talk in the wind. A wolf is
fierce, but he is our brother he lives the old way, but the Sagan-
ash [white man] is sometime a pup and he dies when the wind
blows on him, becase he sees only trees and rocks and water,
only the outside of the book and cant read. We are two hundred
years behind the times and dont change much. . . . I am hunting in a place called Place-where-the-water-runs-in-the-middle
becase the water runs in the center of the lake. . . . It is now
Seegwun when the snow is all melt of the ice and it thaw in the
daytime and freeze at night, making a crust so the moose breaks
through and cant run. This is the days when we have hardship
and our snowshoes break through the crust and get wet and
heavy an our feet is wet everyday all the time wet. The crows
have come back. Between now and the breakup is pleasant
weather in the settlements but it is hell in the woods. White men
dont travel not at all now and I don't blame him. March
20th/18 Well I lay up all day today in my camp and it is a soft
moon, which is bad beleive me, so I write more to your letter. I

travel all day yestdy on the lakes in water and slush half way to my knees on top of the ice. It will be an early spring. My wound has kinda gone on the blink, to hard goin. . . . Well the spring birds waken me up in the morning, but they eat my meat hanging outside too, but they are welcome to it, a long time I didn't see them and I am to glad too be back wher I can get meat and be wher there is birds. . . . I caught a squirrell in a trap by accident I had set for a fisher. He was dead and I felt sorry. I made my dinner in the snow right there an sat an think an smoke an think about it and everything until the wind changed an blow the smoke in my face an I went away then. An I wondered if the tall black trees standing all aroun and the Gweegweechee [whisky-jacks] in the trees and the old men that still travel the woods, thats dead long long ago I wondered if they knowed what I was thinkin about, Me, I kinda forgotten anyhow. Theys a bunch of red birds outside feeding. I guess youd find them pretty, red with stripes on their wings. Well Miss Nurse this is somewheres around the last of March. Half of the snow is went now and the lakes are solid ice about 4 or 3 feet thick. That all has to go in about one month. The sun is getting warm. . . . Did I ever tell you about my throwin knife I had, well I got it back it lays along side of me as I write, the edge all gapped from choppin moose bones with. I would sure like to show you this country with its big waters and black forests an little lonely lakes with a wall of trees all around them, quiet, never move but just look on an on an you know as you go by them trees was there ahead of you an will be there after you are dead. It makes a person feel small, ony with us, that is our life to be among them things. I killed that lynx today and somehow I wisht I hadnt. His skin is only worth $10 an he didnt act cross an the way he looked at me I cant get it out of my mind. I don't think I will sell that skin no. . . . I was on a side hill facing south and in spots it was bare of snow and the leaves were dry under my feet an I thought of what I tol you onct, about bein sick. Once I walked amongst flowers in the spring sun and now I stand on dry leaves an the wind blows cold through the bare tree tops. I think it tells me that wind that pretty soon no one cannot ever hear me. That must be so becase I cannot see my own trail ahead of me. a cloud hangs over it. Away ahead not so awful far the trail goes into the cloud, the sun dies behind the hills, there are no more trees ony the cloud. I had a freind he is dead now. I wonder if he is lonesome. I am now. . . . Hows the wee garden and the nieces coming along. Write and tellme all bout them. My ears are open. . . . I will listen to the song of a bird for a little while. Now the curtain is pulled down across the sun and my heart is black. A singing bird comes and sings an says I do this an I do that an things are so with me an I will lisen an forget there is no sun, until the bird goes, then I will sit and think an smoke for hours an say to my-self, that's good, *I am only an Injun and that bird sang for me.* When the morning wind rises and the morning star hangs off the edge of the black swamp to the east, tomorrow, I will be on my snoeshoe trail. Goodbye.

15 FROM *Theodore Roosevelt*
These Foolish Sentimentalists

This selection by an author who was shortly to become one of the United States' most influential presidents puts the American treatment of Indians in a favorable light, directly opposed to the criticism of Helen Hunt Jackson, whom he named as chief of sentimentalists. Oddly, both he and Mrs. Jackson spoke from personal experience as well as from scholarly knowledge. She had married a banker from Colorado after a genteel upbringing in Amherst, Massachussets. The scion of a prosperous Hudson River family and a graduate of Harvard, he had maintained a ranch in Dakota Territory. Both knew what they were talking about from preconceptions that they might have been expected to share, and yet did not. On the basis of this selection, the reader has little reason to choose between their two arguments. A comparable selection from Mrs. Jackson's A Century of Dishonor *is not included only because it supports the Indian view already documented. The evidence for her views is by no means inferior to that proffered by Roosevelt.*

SOURCE. Theodore Roosevelt, *The Winning of the West*, 4 vols. (New York, 1889–1896) , *I*, pp. 331–335.

The real question facing the reader is how to interpret much the same facts. Although Roosevelt poses as the "realist" here, he was not immune to sentimentality when it came to the Philippine question, at which time he invoked traditional notions of Manifest Destiny, normally accounted sentimental by critical historians. And, yet, if all registers of "fact" depend on underlying preconceptions that are not themselves dependent on experience, the whole faith in education becomes absurd. Either something happens to somebody that makes a difference, or nothing makes a difference. The history of the United States argues for a qualified difference. Classical imperialism took a different direction, of which Roosevelt became a leading spokesman, mediating between continentalism and extracontinental ambition. His contribution here is almost impossible of editorial guidance by way of footnotes unless the reader has a detailed knowledge of Indian history.

It is greatly to be wished that some competent person would write a full and true history of our national dealings with the Indians. Undoubtedly the latter have often suffered terrible injustice at our hands. A number of instances, such as the conduct of the Georgians to the Cherokees in the early part of the present century, or the whole treatment of Chief Joseph and his Nez Perçés,* might be mentioned, which are indelible blots on our fair fame; and yet, in describing our dealings with the red men as a whole, historians do us much less than justice.

It was wholly impossible to avoid conflicts with the weaker race, unless we were willing to see the American continent fall into the hands of some other strong power; and even had we adopted such a ludicrous policy, the Indians themselves would have made war upon us. It cannot be too often insisted that they did not own the land; or, at least, that their ownership was merely such as that claimed often by our own white hunters. If the Indians really owned Kentucky in 1775, then in 1776 it was the

* Refer to Dee Brown's *Bury My Heart at Wounded Knee* for this episode.

property of Boon and his associates; and to dispossess one party
was as great a wrong as to dispossess the other. To recognize the
Indian ownership of the limitless prairies and forests of this continent—that is, to consider the dozen squalid savages who hunted at long intervals over a territory of a thousand square miles as
owning it outright—necessarily implies a similar recognition of
the claims of every white hunter, squatter, horse-thief, or wan-
dering cattle-man. Take as an example the country round the
Little Missouri. When the cattle-men, the first actual settlers,
came into this land in 1882, it was already scantily peopled by a
few white hunters and trappers. The latter were extremely jealous of intrusion; they had held their own in spite of the Indians,
and, like the Indians, the inrush of settlers and the consequent
destruction of the game meant their own undoing; also, again
like the Indians, they felt that their having hunted over the soil
gave them a vague prescriptive right to its sole occupation, and
they did their best to keep actual settlers out. In some cases, to
avoid difficulty, their nominal claims were bought up; generally,
and rightly, they were disregarded. Yet they certainly had as
good a right to the Little Missouri country as the Sioux have to
most of the land on their present reservations. In fact, the mere
statement of the case is sufficient to show the absurdity of assert-
ing that the land really belonged to the Indians. The different
tribes have always been utterly unable to define their own
boundaries. Thus the Delawares and Wyandots, in 1785, though
entirely separate nations, claimed and, in a certain sense, occupied almost exactly the same territory.

Moreover, it was wholly impossible for our policy to be always consistent. Nowadays we undoubtedly ought to break up
the great Indian reservations, disregard the tribal governments,
allot the land in severalty (with, however, only a limited power
of alienation) , and treat the Indians as we do other citizens, with
certain exceptions, for their sakes as well as ours. But this policy,
which it would be wise to follow now, would have been wholly
impracticable a century since. Our central government was then
too weak either effectively to control its own members or adequately to punish aggressions made upon them; and even if it
had been strong, it would probably have proved impossible to

keep entire order over such a vast, sparsely-peopled frontier, with such turbulent elements on both sides. The Indians could not be treated as individuals at that time. There was no possible alternative, therefore, to treating their tribes as nations, exactly as the French and English had done before us. Our difficulies were partly inherited from these, our predecessors, were partly caused by our own misdeeds, but were mainly the inevitable result of the conditions under which the problem had to be solved; no human wisdom or virtue could have worked out a peaceable solution. As a nation, our Indian policy is to be blamed, because of the weakness it displayed, because of its shortsightedness, and its occasional leaning to the policy of the sentimental humanitarians; and we have often promised what was impossible to perform; but there has been little wilful wrong-doing. Our government almost always tried to act fairly by the tribes; the governmental agents (some of whom have been dishonest, and others foolish, but who, as a class, have been greatly traduced), in their reports, are far more apt to be unjust to the whites than to the reds; and the Federal authorities, though unable to prevent much of the injustice, still did check and control the white borders very much more effectually than the Indian sachems and war-chiefs controlled their young braves. The tribes were warlike and bloodthirsty, jealous of each other and of the whites; they claimed the land for their hunting grounds, but their claims all conflicted with one another; their knowledge of their own boundaries was so indefinite that they were always willing, for inadequate compensation, to sell land to which they had merely the vaguest title; and yet, when once they had received the goods, were generally reluctant to make over even what they could; they coveted the goods and scalps of the whites, and the young warriors were always on the altert to commit outrages when they could do it with impunity. On the other hand, the evil-disposed whites regarded the Indians as fair game for robbery and violence of any kind; and the far larger number of well-disposed men, who would not willingly wrong any Indian, were themselves maddened by the memories of hideous injuries received. They bitterly resented the action of the government, which, in their eyes, failed to properly protect them, and yet sought to keep them out of waste, uncultivated lands which they did not regard as being any more the property of the Indians than of their own hunters. With the best intentions, it was wholly impossible for any government to evolve order out of such a chaos without resort to the ultimate arbitrator—the sword.

The purely sentimental historians take no account of the difficulties under which we labored, nor of the countless wrongs and provocations we endured, while grossly magnifying the already lamentably large number of injuries for which we really deserve to be held responsible. To get a fair idea of the Indians of the present day, and of our dealings with them, we have fortunately one or two excellent books, notably "Hunting Grounds of the Great West," and "Our Wild Indians," by Col. Richard I. Dodge (Hartford, 1882), and "Massacres of the Mountains," by J. P. Dunn (New York, 1886). As types of the opposite class, which are worse than valueless, and which nevertheless might cause some hasty future historian, unacquainted with the facts, to fall into grievous error, I may mention, "A Century of Dishonor," by H. H. (Mrs. Helen Hunt Jackson), and "Our Indian Wards," (Geo. W. Manypenny). The latter is a mere spiteful diatribe against various army officers, and neither its manner nor its matter warrants more than an allusion. Mrs. Jackson's book is capable of doing more harm because it is written in good English, and because the author, who had lived a pure and noble life, was intensely in earnest in what she wrote, and had the most praiseworthy purpose—to prevent our committing any more injustice to the Indians. This was all most proper; every good man or woman should do whatever is possible to make the government treat the Indians of the present time in the fairest and most generous spirit, and to provide against any repetition of such outrages as were inflicted upon the Nez Percés and upon part of the Cheyennes,* or the wrongs with which the civilized nations of the Indian territory are sometimes threatened. The purpose of the book is excellent, but the spirit in which it is written cannot be called even technically honest. As a polemic, it is possible that it did not do harm (though the effect of even a polemic is marred by hysterical indifference to facts.) As a history it would be beneath criticism, were it not that the high character of the

* See Dee Brown, op. cit., for this reference.

author and her excellent literary work in other directions have given it a fictitious value and made it much quoted by the large class of amiable but maudlin fanatics concerning whom it may be said that the excellence of their intentions but indifferently atones for the invariable folly and ill effect of their actions. It is not too much to say that the book is thoroughly untrustworthy from cover to cover, and that not a single statement it conains should be acceped without independent proof; for even those that are not absolutely false, are often as bad on account of so much of the truth having been suppressed. One effect of this is of course that the author's recitals of the many real wrongs of Indian tribes utterly fail to impress us, because she lays quite as much stress on those that are non-existent, and on the equally numerous cases where the wrong-doing was wholly the other way. To get an idea of the value of the work, it is only necessary to compare her statements about almost any tribe with the real facts, choosing at random; for instance, compare her accounts of the Sioux and the plains tribes generally, with those given by Col. Dodge in his two books; or her recital of the Sandy Creek massacre with the facts as stated by Mr. Dunn—who is apt, if any thing, to lean to the Indian's side.

These foolish sentimentialists not only write foul slanders about their own countrymen, but are themselves the worst possible advisers on any point touching Indian management. They would do well to heed General Sheridan's bitter words, written when many Easterners were clamoring against the army authorities because they took partial vengenance for a series of brutal outrages: "I do not know how far these humanitarians should be excused on account of their ignorance; but surely it is the only excuse that can give a shadow of justification for aiding and abetting such horrid crimes."

PART FOUR

The Civilization Trust

QUOTABLE QUOTES

"The *New-Englanders* are a People of God settled in those, which were once the *Devils* Territories; and it may easily be supposed that the *Devil* was Exceedingly disturbed, when he perceived such a People here accomplishing the Promise of old made unto our Blesed Jesus. *That He should have the Utmost parts of the Earth for his Possession.*"

Cotton Mather, 1693

"The far-reaching, the boundless future will be the era of American greatness. In its magnificent domain of space and time, the nation of many nations is destined to manifest to mankind the excellence of divine principles; to establish on earth the noblest temple ever dedicated to the worship of the Most High —the Sacred and the True. Its floor shall be a hemisphere—its roof the firmament of the star-studded heavens, and its congregation an Union of many Republics, comprising hundreds of happy millions, calling, owning no man master, but governed by God's natural and moral law of equality, the law of brotherhood—of 'peace and good will amongst men.'

John L. O'Sullivan, 1839

" 'Well, sir!' cried the war correspondent, 'since you have concluded to call upon me, I will respond. I will respond. I will give you, sir, The Rowdy Journal and its brethren [a toast]; the

93

well of Truth, whose waters are black from being composed of printers' ink, but are quite clear enough for my country to behold the shadow of her Destiny reflected in.'

" 'Hear, hear!' cried the colonel, with great complacency. 'There are flowery components, sir, in the language of my friend?' [Turning to his guest, Martin Chuzzlewit]

" 'Very much so, indeed,' said Martin.

" ' There is to-day's Rowdy, sir,' observed the colonel, handing him a paper. 'You'll find Jefferson Brick at his usual post in the van of human civilisation and moral purity.' "

Charles Dickens, 1844

"The Mediterranean era died with the discovery of America; the Atlantic era is now at the height of its development and must soon exhaust the resources at its command; the Pacific era is destined to be the greatest of all, is just at its dawn."

Theodore Roosevelt, 1902

16 FROM Charles Sumner
A Future Dominion in the Pacific

Charles Sumner, ardent foe of slavery, from Massachusetts, led the fight in the Senate for Alaska in this speech, from which is omitted only his historical introduction about negotiations with Russia and his later appended information derived in a scholarly fashion from sailing captains since Captain Cooke, early American entrepreneurs in Alaska, and one official expedition that had not completed its report at the time of his original speech on the Senate floor. An interesting sidelight is that some of his information came from an abortive enterprise to string a telegraphic line from Alaska across Siberia to the capitals of Europe. This enterprise folded with the successful laying of an underwater Atlantic cable. Notable about this speech is Sumner's recognition, long before 1898, that Alaska represented a break with continental traditions—hence his caveat. The acquisition of Alaska was the prelude to overseas expansion. His caveat stemmed from an initial reluctance to become involved in a seemingly imperialistic venture, a reluctance overcome only by his warm friendship with William H. Seward, President Lincoln's and Johnson's Secretary of State.

SOURCE. *Speech of Hon. Charles Sumner of Massachusetts on the Cession of Russian America to the United States, April 9, 1867* (Washington, D. C., 1867), *passim;* reprinted in Charles Sumner's *Works,* XI (Boston, 1875), pp. 216–232.

1. *Advantages to the Pacific Coast*. Foremost in order, if not in importance, I put the desires of our fellow-citizens on the Pacific coast, and the special advantages they will derive from this enlargement of boundary. They were the first to ask for it, and will be the first to profit by it. . . .

These well-known desires were founded, of course, on supposed advantages; and here experience and neighborhood were prompters. Since 1854 the people of California have received their ice from the freshwater lakes in the island of Kadiak, not far westward from Mount St. Elias. Later still, their fishermen have searched the waters about the Aleutians and the Shumagins, commencing a promising fishery. Others have proposed to substitute themselves for the Hudson's Bay Company in their franchise on the coast. But all are looking to the Orient, as in the time of Columbus, although like him they sail to the west. To them China and Japan, those ancient realms of fabulous wealth, are the Indies. . . .

The absence of harbors belonging to the United States on the Pacific limits the outlets of the country. On that whole extent, from Panama to Puget Sound, the only harbor of any considerable value is San Francisco. Further north the harbors are abundant, and they are all nearer to the great marts of Japan and China. But San Francisco itself will be nearer by the way of the Aleutians than by Honolulu. . . .

The advantages to the Pacific coast have two aspects,—one domestic, and the other foreign. Not only does the treaty extend the coasting trade of California, Oregon, and Washington Territory northward, but it also extends the base of commerce with China and Japan.

To unite the East of Asia with the West of America is the aspiration of commerce now as when the English navigator recorded his voyage. Of course, whatever helps this result is an advantage. The Pacific Railroad is such an advantage; for, though running westward, it will be, when completed, a new highway to the East. This treaty is another advantage; for nothing can be clearer than that the western coast must exercise an attraction which will be felt in China and Japan just in proportion as it is occupied by a commercial people communicating readily with the Atlantic and with Europe. This cannot be without consequences not less important politically than commercially. Owing so much to the Union, the people there will be bound to it anew, and the national unity will receive another confirmation. Thus the whole country will be a gainer. So are we knit together that the advantages to the Pacific coast will contribute to the general welfare.

2. *Extension of Dominion.* The extension of dominion is another consideration calculated to captivate the public mind. . . .

The passion for acquisition, so strong in the individual, is not less strong in the community. A nation seeks an outlying territory, as an individual seeks an outlying farm. . . . It is common to the human family. There are few anywhere who could hear of a considerable accession of territory, obtained peacefully and honestly, without a pride of country, even if at certain moments the judgment hesitated. With increased size on the map there is increased consciousness of strength, and the heart of the citizen throbs anew as he traces the extending line.

3. *Extension of Republican Institutions.* More than the extension of dominion is the extension of republican institutions, which is a traditional aspiration. . . .

John Adams, in the preface to his Defense of the American Constitutions . . . thus for a moment lifts the curtain: "Thirteen governments," he says plainly, "thus founded on the natural authority of the people alone, without a pretence of miracle or mystery, and *which are destined to spread over the northern part of that whole quarter of the globe,* are a great point gained in favor of the rights of mankind." . . .

By the text of our Constitution, the United States are bound to guaranty "a republican form of government" to every State in the Union; but this obligation, which is applicable only at home, is an unquestionable indication of the national aspiration everywhere. The Republic is something more than a local policy; it is a general principle, not to be forgotten at any time, especially when the opportunity is presented of bringing an immense region within its influence. . . .

The present treaty is a visible step in the occupation of the whole North American continent. As such it will be recognized by the world and accepted by the American people. But the treaty involves something more. We dismiss one other monarch from the continent. One by one they have retired,—first France, then Spain, then France again, and now Russia,—all giving way to the absorbing Unity declared in the national motto, *E pluribus unum.*

4. *Anticipation of Great Britain.* Another motive to this acquisition may be found in the desire to anticipate imagined schemes or necessties of Great Britain. With regard to all these I confess doubt; and yet, if we credit report, it would seem as if there were already a British movement in this direction. . . .

5. *Amity of Russia.* There is still another consideration concerning this treaty not to be disregarded. It attests and assures the amity of Russia. Even if you doubt the value of these possessions, the treaty is a sign of friendship. It is a new expression of that *entente cordiale* between the two powers which is a phenomenon of history. Though unlike in institutions, they are not unlike in recent experience. Sharers of common glory in a great act of Emancipation, they also share together the opposition or antipathy of other nations. Perhaps this experience has not been without effect in bringing them together. At all events, no coldness or unkindness has interfered at any time with their good relations. . . .

A CAVEAT

But there is one other point on which I file my caveat. This treaty must not be a precedent for a system of indiscriminate and costly annexation. Sincerely believing that republican institutions under the primacy of the United States must embrace this whole continent, I cannot adopt the sentiment of Jefferson, who, while confessing satisfaction in settlements on the Pacific coast, saw there in the future nothing but "free and independent Americans," bound to the United States only by "ties of blood and interest" without political unity. Nor am I willing to restrain myself to the principle so tersely expressed by Andrew Jackson, in his letter to President Monroe: "Concentrate our population, confine our frontier to proper limits, until our country, to those limits, is filled with a dense population." But I cannot disguise my anxiety that every state in our predestined future shall be by natural processes without war, and I would add, even without purchase. There is no territorial aggrandizement which is worth the price of blood. Only under peculiar circumstances can it become the subject of pecuniary contract. Our triumph should be by growth and organic expanison in obedience to "pre-established harmony," recognizing always the will of those who are to become our fellow-citizens. All this must be easy if we are only true to ourselves. Our motto may be that of Goethe, "Without haste, without rest." Let the republic be assured in tranquil liberty with all equal before the law, and it will conquer by its sublime example. . . . Plant it with schools; cover it with churches; fill it with libraries; make it abundant with comfort so that poverty shall disappear; keep it constant in the assertion of human rights. And here we may fitly recall those words of antiquity, which Cicero quoted from the Greek, and which Webster in our day quoted from Cicero: "You have a Sparta; adorn it."

17   FROM   *Editorial Opinion*
Was Alaska "Seward's Folly"?

Contrary to an enduring historical myth, the great majority of newspaper editors throughout the nation supported Seward's purchase of Alaska, many of them, as the sampling of editorial opinion below suggests, with the enthusiastic rhetoric of Manifest Destiny. Although the New York Herald, *for instance, ridiculed Seward's "dinner diplomacy," it heartily approved of the purchase itself. There was also the scandal of bribery attached to the treaty's ratification for which a few editors held Seward responsible.*

SOURCES. (1) The Chicago *Evening Journal* for April 1, 1867. (2) The New York *World* for April 1, 1867. (3) The Victoria (B. C.) *Colonist* for May 16, 1867. (4) The New York *Daily Tribune* for April 11, 1867 and July 16, 1868. (5) The New York *Herald* for April 9, 1867.

1.

The acquisition of Russian America by the United States has the promise of future good. . . . The paltry sum of $7,000,000 for a country nearly eight times as large as this state [Illinois] and 400 miles of coast, shows Russia has some ulterior object to gain. . . . [It] more than doubles our Pacific Coast, yet adds but little to the productive territory of the nation. Russian America is a dreary waste of snow and ice. . . . Its military importance is its chief value, although its commercial significance may become, eventually, very great. The commerce of the Pacific has not been developed to any considerable extent, but it is destined to pass and perhaps rival, and probably surpass, that of the Atlantic. This cession of Russian America will probably help us materially in controlling that commerce. . . . The effect of this cession will also be to hasten the time when British Columbia will become a part of the United States. The colonists themselves have already taken the initial steps in the direction of annexation and being surrounded by the United States will tend to strengthen and tighten the cords that were already drawing that province into the folds of the American Union. . . .

It must also be admitted that while the Secretary of State stumbles and blunders egregiously on domestic policies, he is a consummate master of diplomacy, and manages our foreign affairs with matchless wisdom. It would not be strange if this last great act of his life should prove so eminently beneficial that his charitable countrymen will yet pass over his derelictions in silence, remembering only the good he has done. However this may be, it is quite certain that a new and inestimably important page has been turned in the history of the United States by the acquisition of the Russian possessions in America.

2.

Russia has sold us a sucked orange. Whatever may be the value of that territory and its outlying islands to us, it has ceased to be of any to Russia. The only way she ever did, or ever could, utilize the northwest coast was in the prosecution of the fur trade. But that trade has declined and nearly run out by the destruction of the animals (particularly the Otter), which have been hunted so industriously that not enough were left to breed and keep up the race. What remains of the Russian fur trade is not of sufficient importance to justify the expense of the naval protection required by the establishments. Russia has therefore done wisely in selling the territory and islands which to her had become useless.

But have we done wisely in buying it? If estimated by what it is in itself, certainly not, if by what the purchase may hereafter lead to, perhaps yes.

When Franklin was asked the use of some new discovery in science, his reply was: "What is the use of a newborn infant? It may become a man." It is only in some such prospective view that we can discover any value in this new purchase. It is almost amusing to read the comments of the effervescing quidnuncs who first heralded the news. They dilate on the vastness of the territory—ten or twelve times as large, they say, as the State of New York. But the greater part of it is of no more value for any human use than so many square miles of ice in the Arctic Ocean by which it is bounded. . . . Other explosive enthusiasts think the purchase opens brilliant prospects for the China and Japan trade! As the territory can never have a population of consumers, and lies at a vast distance from the route for supplying inhabited countries, it is not very obvious how the new acquisition is to contribute mightily to the development of the Asiatic trade. . . . The small value of the territory in itself being so evident to everyone who will make the effort to look into the subject, its purchase, at the price paid, is not defensible except with a view to ulterior objects. . . .

The purchase of the Russian territory renders it morally certain that we shall some day acquire [British Columbia].

In the first place, a gap in our possessions on the Pacific Coast will always be an eye-sore to the nation, whose sense of symmetry will be offended by the ragged look of the maps. The national imagination shall always require that our coast line shall be continuous, and this aspiration will sooner or later be potential. It will secure for the government efficient popular support whenever the time shall be ripe for completing what is now begun.

The acquisition [of the territory] is important because the British part of the coast is certain to follow at some day more or less remote. So long as the two nations are at peace, we can take no other steps toward its acquisition than proposals to purchase. If such proposals are rejected, we can afford to wait, since time will accomplish much for us and nothing for Great Britain. Our population and military strength on the Pacific are growing so rapidly that the seizure of the residue of the coast in the event of war, will become constantly easier. If we should never have another war with Great Britain, we shall never need the territory. If we should have a war, we shall of course take it.

Looking to the future, we must regard the purchase of the Russian possessions as wise, although they are of little immediate value. It is an advancing step in that manifest destiny which is yet to give us British North America. When we have completed our coast line on the Pacific, we shall have hemmed around and shut in from the sea nearly the whole British territory. Canada lies behind our New England States, and New York, which form a broad belt separating it from the Atlantic. The St. Lawrence River is of little value as an outlet, because it is closed by ice a great part of the year, and its mouth enveloped with fogs which render navigation dangerous even during the warm season. A country thus shut in would find itself so crippled if we should close our gates, that its people will in time be convinced that annexation is for their interest.

3.

Here on Vancouver Island, within a few degrees of the recently acquired tract, we are in a position to state that it is a most valuable acquisition, and that its cession to the United States is likely to inflict a serious blow to British interest in the Pacific, if not exercise an unfavorable influence upon the whole of British North America. The purchase was a master-stroke on the part of Mr. Seward.

By it the United States virtually secures control of the Coast, opens a new field for American enterprise and capital, and places the whole of Her Majesty's possession on this coast in the position of a piece of meat between two slices of bread, where they may be devoured at a single bite.

The moral effect of this purchase has been to dissipate the rose-

colored pictures we have painted of the future of British institutions on this coast, and to increase popular discontent with a
government that has done so little to encourage this young colony.

The imbecility, ignorance or neglect of British statesmen has
allowed a glorious opportunity to pass unimproved and has left
the colony of British Columbia so closely hemmed in by her colossal neighbors that she has scarcely room left to draw a long
breath.

4.

We simply obtain by the treaty the nominal possession of im-
passable deserts of snow, vast tracts of dwarf timbers, frozen rivers, inaccessible mountain ranges, with a few islands where the
climate is more moderate, and a scanty population supported by
fishing and trading with the Indians. Virtually we get, by an expenditure of seven millions in gold, Sitka and the Prince of
Wales Islands. All the rest is waste territory, and no energy of
the American people will be sufficient to make mining specula-
tions in the 60th degree north latitude profitable, or to reclaim
wildernesses which border on the Arctic Ocean. We may make a
treaty with Russia but we cannot make a treaty with the North
Wind, or the Snow King. Ninety-nine hundredths of Russian
America are absolutely useless; the remaining hundredth may be
of some value to the Russians who settled it, but it certainly is
not worth seven millions of dollars to a nation already possessed
of more territory than it can decently govern, and burdened with
debt. . . . The expense and trouble of a territorial government
. . . in this distant and uninhabitable land, would far outweigh
any advantage from its codfish or bear skins. To Russia it was an
encumberance; to us it would be an embarrassment and by the
next session of Congress we trust the folly of the purchase will be
made so plain that the House will refuse to make the necessary
appropriation.

When the question of ratifying the treaty remained undecided
in the Senate, we did our best to defeat ratification. Beaten there,
we have not felt justified in urging the House to refuse the re-

quisite appropriation. We believe it was advisable to pay the money. Having received it (the money) we wish Russia would consent to receive back the territory as a free gift from this Republic. We should deem it a very happy riddance.

Of course we readily agree that there are fish swimming around the isles that are included in our hard bargain. There is timber on the Yukon and its southern tributaries. There may be gold and silver—anything you please under the Alaskan snows and mosses. But they who catch the fish, or cut the timber, or dig the gold, will keep it for their trouble as is right. They will dearly earn all they get. We the people of the United States must pay the $7,200,000 purchase money, and survey the coasts, (there are thousands of miles in all) and dig out the harbors, and build the forts and construct the piers, and erect the light houses, etc. Taxes! Taxes! Taxes! even more and heavier taxes! That is our part in the great acquisition. Our elephant is costly and clumsy; and Oh, such an appetite!

5.

Mr. Seward, they say, is working like a beaver, or rather like a whole colony of beavers, to get his Russian American treaty through the Senate. . . . [It is reported that] Seward's chances with his Esquimax acquisition treaty are improving daily . . . that the industrious Premier is working the telegraphs and the Associated Press in the manufacture of public opinion night and day, and that he has likewise, two other machines running off the same material, a yard wide, at ten cents a yard. These two machines, high pressure, oscillating engines, are first, the Secretary's dinners and second, the Washington lobby, strengthened by some of the most skillful graduates of the old Fagin of Albany.

These vultures have discovered that there is money in this thing, and they are hungry for a sop in those seven millions of American gold for Russian icebergs. Mr. Seward's dinner table is spread first with a map of Russian America, and this cloth is covered with "roast treaty, boiled treaty, treaty in bottles, treaty in decanters, treaties garnishd with with appointments to office, treaty in statistics[Thurlow Weed's], treaty clad in furs, ornamented with walrus teeth, fringed with timber and flopping with fish." In short, Mr. Seward's dinner diplomacy is said to have worked such wonders among the conscript fathers of the Senate that "the Esquimaux ring" are ready to bet their pile on Seward and Mt. St. Elias on a test vote.

18 FROM *House Debate on the Alaskan Appropriation Bill The Capital of the World*

These brief excerpts from speeches by Representative Raum of Illinois and Representative Donelly of Minnesota suggest that the long view of destiny prevailed over considerations of immediate commercial advantage in the final vote for funding this treaty.

1.

The day will come when the Pacific will be our greatest stronghold, and when that day arrives, those responsible for the building and maintaining of the necessary defense depots will bless the memory of those whose courage and foresight have caused them to vote for the confirmation of this treaty.

2.

Let us then not put aside this acquisition. Our flag now floats over it. That flag should never recede. Let us take this territory for its present worth—its soil, its harbors, its fisheries, furs and forests,—not over-rating them but remembering that there is always a tendency of the mind to undervalue all unknown lands. But beyond all the present importance of this region let its future consequence be recognized. The entire Pacific Coast of the North American continent fronting Japan, China and India

SOURCE. The full context is found in the *Congressional Globe*, 40th Congress, 2nd Session, Vol. IV, 3625–27, 3659–60, 4054; Vol. V, Appendix, 386–432.

should belong to the nation whose capital is here, and whose destiny it is to grasp the commerce of all the seas and sway the sceptre of the world. Let us then, while perfecting our institutions, not refuse to extend our boundaries.

19   FROM   *Alfred Thayer Mahan*
A Twentieth-Century Outlook

As the following selection demonstrates, Admiral Mahan (1840–1914) was something more and less than the great ideologue of naked power that he has been reputed to be. That is, although he did, indeed, think on a large world scale of geopolitics and insist that national objectives be supported by all necessary means to their achievement, particularly sea power, his consuming interest and reason for expending his energies on such analysis lay in the ideal—what he conceived to be the civilizing mission of America. The grand design that he sketches here needed only the Spanish-American War to give it life. More than any other single person, he set the stage for that war—and in this work; a set of fortuitous (and quite unexpected) circumstances, seized on by influential readers of Mahan who were themselves captives of Manifest Destiny, supplied the actors for the stage. Here, once again we observe, as with the acquisition of Alaska, that America's paramount interest in the Caribbean and Central America was related to the traditional polarity of the East and the West with an eye on the farther reaches of the Pacific.

In the determination of the duties of nations, nearness is the most conspicuous and the most general indication. Considering the American states as members of the European family, as they are by traditions, institutions, and languages, it is in the Pacific,

SOURCE. Alfred T. Mahan, *The Interest of America in Sea Power, Present and Future* (Boston, 1897) , pp. 259–268.

where the westward course of empire again meets the East, that
their relations to the future of the world become most apparent.
The Atlantic, bordered on either shore by the European family
in the strongest and most advanced types of its political development, no longer severs, but binds together, by all the facilities
and abundance of water communications, the once divided children of the same mother; the inheritors of Greece and Rome,
and of the Teutonic conquerors of the latter. A limited express
or a flying freight may carry a few passengers or a small bulk
overland from the Atlantic to the Pacific more rapidly than modern steamers can cross the former ocean, but for the vast
amounts in numbers or in quantity which are required for the
full fruition of communication, it is the land that divides, and not
the sea. On the Pacific coast, severed from their brethren by desert and mountain range, are found the outposts, the exposed pioneers of European civilization, whom it is one of the first duties
of the European family to bind more closely to the main body,
and to protect, by due foresight over the approaches to them on
either side.

It is in this political fact, and not in the weighing of merely
commercial advantages, that is to be found the great significance
of the future canal across the Central American isthmus, as well
as the importance of the Caribbean Sea; for the latter is insepara-
bly intwined with all international considertion of the isthmus
problem. Wherever situated, whether at Panama or at Nicaragua, the fundamental meaning of the canal will be that it advances by thousands of miles the frontiers of European civilization in general, and of the United States in particular; that it
knits together the whole system of American states enjoying that
civilization as in no other way they can be bound. In the Caribbean Archipelago—the very domain of sea power, if ever region
could be called so—are the natural home and centre of those influences by which such a maritime highway as a canal must be
controlled, even as the control of the Suez Canal rests in the
Mediterranean. Hawaii, too, is an outpost of the canal, as surely
as Aden or Malta is of Suez; or as Malta was of India in the
days long before the canal, when Nelson proclaimed that in that
point of view chiefly was it important to Great Britain. In the
cluster of island fortresses of the Caribbean is one of the greatest

of the nerve centres of the whole body of European civilization; and it is to be regretted that so serious a portion of them now is in hands which not only never have given, but to all appearances never can give, the development which is required by the general interest. . . .

On the side of the sea there is no state charged with weightier responsibilities than the United States. In the Caribbean, the sensitive resentment by our people of any supposed fresh encroachment by another state of the European family has been manifested too plainly and too recently to admit of dispute. Such an attitude of itself demands of us to be ready to support it by organized force, exactly as the mutual jealousy of states within the European Continent imposes upon them the maintenance of their great armies—destined, we believe, in the future, to fulfil a nobler mission. Where we thus exclude others, we accept for ourselves the responsibility for that which is due to the general family of our civilization; and the Caribbean Sea, with its isthmus, is the nexus where will meet the chords binding the East to the West, the Atlantic to the Pacific.

The Isthmus, with all that depends upon it,—its canal and its approaches on either hand,—will link the eastern side of the American continent to the western as no network of land communications ever can. In it the United States has asserted a special interest. In the present she can maintain her claim, and in the future perform her duty, only by the creation of that sea power upon which predominance in the Caribbean must ever depend. In short, as the internal jealousies of Europe, and the purely democratic institution of the *levée en masse*—the general enforcement of military training—have prepared the way for great national armies, whose mission seems yet obscure, so the gradual broadening and tightening hold upon the sentiment of American democracy of that conviction loosely characterized as the Monroe doctrine finds its logical and inevitable outcome in a great sea power, the correlative, in connection with that of Great Britain, of those armies which continue to flourish under the most popular institutions, despite the wails of economists and the lamentations of those who wish peace without paying the one price which alone has ever insured peace,—readiness for war.

Thus it was, while readiness for war lasted, that the Teuton was held back until he became civilized, humanized, after the standard of that age; till the root of the matter was in him, sure to bear fruit in due season. He was held back by organized armed force—by armies. Will it be said that that was in a past barbaric age? Barbarism, however, is not in more or less material prosperity, or even political development, but in the inner man, in the spiritual ideal; and the material, which comes first and has in itself no salt of life to save from corruption, must be controlled by other material forces, until the spiritual can find room and time to germinate. We need not fear but that that which appeals to the senses in our civilization will be appropriated, even though it be necessary to destroy us, if disarmed, in order to obtain it. Our own civilization less its spiritual element is barbarism; and barbarism will be the civilizaton of those who assimilate its material progress without imbibing the indwelling spirit.

Let us worship peace, indeed, as the goal at which humanity must hope to arrive; but let us not fancy that peace is to be had as a boy wrenches an unripe fruit from a tree. Nor will peace be reached by ignoring the conditions that confront us, or by exaggerating the charms of quiet, of prosperity, of ease, and by contrasting these exclusively with the alarms and horrors of war. Merely utilitarian arguments have never convinced nor converted mankind, and they never will; for mankind knows that there is something better. Its homage will never be commanded by peace, presented as the tutelary deity of the stock-market.

Nothing is more ominous for the future of our race than that tendency, vociferous at present, which refuses to recognize in the profession of arms, in war, that something which inspired Wordsworth's "Happy Warrior," which soothed the dying hours of Henry Lawrence, who framed the ideals of his career on the poet's conception, and so nobly illustrated it in his self-sacrifice; that something which has made the soldier to all ages the type of heroism and of self-denial.* When the religion of Christ, of Him

* A dubious example to parade before Americans and to link with Christ. He was heroic enough, but died in the Sepoy Rebellion a martyr to British imperialism in India.

who was led as a lamb to the slaughter, seeks to raise before its followers the image of self-control, and of resistance to evil, it is the soldier whom it presents. He Himself, if by office King of Peace, is, first of all, in the essence of His Being, King of Righteousness, without which true peace cannot be.

Conflict is the condition of all life, material and spiritual; and it is to the soldier's experience that the spiritual life goes for its most vivid metapors nd its loftiest inspirations. Whatever else the twentieth century may bring us, it will not, from anything now current in the thought of the nineteenth, receive a nobler ideal.

20   FROM   *Benjamin Kidd*
The United States and the Control of
the Tropics

As an ideologue, Benjamin Kidd (1858–1916) may justly be considered the British counterpart of Admiral Mahan. He began his career in Her Majesty's Inland Revenue Service, but soon won reknown as an author, world traveler, lecturer, and social philosopher who vied with Herbert Spencer and Thomas Huxley in relating the doctrine of evolution to human affairs. He delivered the Herbert Spencer lectures at Oxford in 1908. His best known work, The Control of the Tropics, *greatly influenced the English statesman, Joseph Chamberlain, and subsequently British colonial policy; this book aroused so much interest in the United States that he was invited to write this article for the* Atlantic Monthly *which, in the tradition of Bishop Berkeley's poem, gave much comfort to Americans who thought of themselves as leading a world movement. In this article, Kidd explicitly places American Manifest Destiny within a world movement.*

If this support of expansionary American nationalism by a "foreigner" seems surprising after more than a century of power-

SOURCE. Benjamin Kidd, "The United States and the Control of the Tropics," *Atlantic Monthly*, LXXXII (1898), pp. 721–727.

*ful antiforeign sentiment, one should be reminded that it oc-
curred during a conciliatory period with England when some of
the best minds in both countries were agitating for an "English-
speaking Union" as the trustee for civilization throughout the
world. What especially attracted Americans to Kidd's ideas was
his justification of imperialistic ambition without the taint of co-
lonialism or simple exploitation. What emerges here is a complex
imperial design which has played too easily into the hands of
American historians who have argued that Manifest Destiny and
imperialism are two very different things.*

The editor of The Atlantic Monthly has written me the following letter:

"In your suggestive volume on the control of the tropics you
declare it futile that any first-class world-power should hope in
the future to fold its hands and stand aloof from the tropics. You
say that there can be no choice in the matter, and that with the
filling up of the temperate regions and the continued development of industrialism, rivalry for the trade of the tropics will be
the largest factor in the era upon which we are entering. You declare that, by reason of past experience, we have now come face
to face with the following conclusions regarding the tropics:

" 'The ethical development that has taken place in our civilization has rendered the experiment once made to develop their
resources by forced native labor no longer possible, or permissi-
ble, even if possible.'

" 'We have already abandoned, under pressure of experience,
the idea, which at one time prevailed, that the tropical regions
might be occupied and permanently colonized by European
races, as vast regions in the temperate climes have been.'

" 'Within a measurable period in the future, and under pressure of experience, we shall probably also have to abandon the
idea, which has in like manner prevailed for a time, that the colored races, left to themselves, possess the qualities necessary to
the development of the rich resources of the lands they have inherited.'

"The only method left, therefore, in your opinion, is that the tropics must be governed from a base in the temperate regions; and, in particular,—and in this you make a new departure,—be governed by the nations which undertake such work *as a trust for civilization*. This solution of the problem of the tropics Great Britain has begun to make in the case of Egypt. But Great Britain is already a world-wide empire, and has developed by long experience the methods and machinery for exercising such control.

"You refrain, in your book on the control of the tropics,—no doubt purposely,—from saying whether, in your judgment, the United States has incurred obligations by her victory over Spain to take a share in the development of the tropics, and whether the United States is politically able to enter upon such a career. The body of opinion in the United States that opposes a policy of expansion bases its objections on these three propositions: (1) that the traditions of the United States are directly and strongly opposed to a policy of expansion, and have been so opposed from George Washington's Farewell Address to the present time; (2) that a dangerous if not an insuperable practical difficulty to a policy of expansion is found in the inefficient civil service of the United States; and (3) that the control of colonies is illogical for the United States, because such a policy directly contradicts the fundamental proposition on which the republican form of government rests,—that it shall consist only of self-governing commonwealths. In view of these objections, do you hold that the United States could safely enter upon a policy of expansion?"

The questions asked in this letter are so very important, and bear so closely upon a great public issue about which it is the right and duty of the people of the United States alone to express a direct opinion, that I feel some difficulty in replying to them. Let me take the propositions in order, and deal first with the policy of expansion. I have recently been traveling over a large part of the United States, particularly in the West. I have been as far west as the Pacific coast, passing over two main lines of communication, out one way and back another, stopping at various places, and living amongst the people a good deal. On this subject of expansion I talked with the people generally. It was impossible to avoid the subject. I was struck by two great bodies of opinion, as I might call them, on the question of expansion. One of these I might describe as being a sort of unreasoning body of opinion; that is to say, it has not been reasoned out. It takes the shape in the popular mind of a pronounced and even intense feeling that in this matter of expansion the duty of the United States is clear. Ask the farmers and business men in the West why the course which they propose is the duty of America. They will give no direct reason or logical reason, as far as I could find out. But they are, nevertheless, perfectly decided about one thing, and that is "that this thing has got to be done." You ask, "What thing?" and they reply, "Why, that America should keep a stiff upper lip to the world; should hold that which she has not sought, but which has come to her; should keep what she has got." She must, in short, in a favorite phrase, be "true to her own destiny."

Now that is one body of opinion. There is also another great body of opinion, largely prevailing amongst the reasoning classes in the United States. Many men of this class undoubtedly hold strongly that the government is about to embark upon a very responsible experiment,—perhaps an experiment in which there is a considerable element of danger.

With regard to the first body of opinion, which is a serious force it seemed to me in most places, I tried to explain to myself what this feeling is which finds expression as "the destiny of America" now to be carried forward in a policy of expansion. I can only put the matter in the shape in which it has presented itself to my own mind. . . .

To take up the threads we must go a little distance back to where we find Spain confronting England in Elizabethan times, with apparently an overwhelming advantage on the side of the former country. Slowly the outwardly stronger power goes down, and toward the end of the eighteenth century it is France, with Spain behind her, which stands confronting England throughout the world. Even yet historians have scarcely fathomed the meaning of the great struggle that culminated in what is known as the Napoleonic wars. Up to recent times Professor Seeley has probably been the only English historian who has risen to the philosophical position of seeing that that contest was in reality a duel, in which France, with Spain behind her, had joined with England for the future of the world,—a duel in which the real issue was whether Latin civilization or that kind of civilization with which England had become identified was to be predominant. The whole Napoleonic era, as Seeley puts it, was but a struggle against the world-expansion of the English principle, and "Napoleon tried to conquer the whole continent of Europe because he realized that he could not otherwise conquer England."

The cost of the conflict to England was enormous. It is impossible to give figures which would bring home to the mind the real extent of the sacrifices made. Toward the close of the war Great Britain's population was about 17,000,000. But before peace was restored that comparatively small nation, at a period when money was very scarce and of higher value than it is now, had incurred a national debt of about $4,000,000,000.

It is not yet perceived in America that one of the principal results of this prolonged struggle has been, not the secession of the United States from England, which was but an incident and of the nature of a development, but rather that the North American continent of the present day speaks English, and not French; and that the immense inheritance of that continent belongs to the type of civilization which the United States now represents, and not to any other type.

But to present the history of this development in its next chapter we have to take a large canvas; for it is necessary to find room for the whole North American continent. Looking at the map of North America immediately before the period when the United States began its career as a nation, we have a remarkable spectacle. A little fringe of English-speaking people, some 5,000,000 in number, occupied the territory along the Atlantic seaboard. The French occupied the broad *hinterland* of the Mississippi Valley. The Spaniards were in possession in the south; they held also the great territories along the Pacific seaboard. This English-speaking territory is little more than a patch on the map, surrounded by territories belonging to one or other of almost all the leading powers of Europe. Yet we look again toward the end of the nineteenth century, and a wonderful transformation has taken place; a later and vaster chapter of the world-movement, of which we had the opening chapters in another hemisphere, has been enacted. North, south, west, from Atlantic to Pacific, from seaboard to seaboard, the great wave of English-speaking civilization has flowed, submerging, nay, obliterating all other forms. Not a square mile of territory, once won, has ever been given back. The meaning of Washington's Farewell Address, delivered when the United States contained only about 6,000,000 people, surrounded on every side by hostile powers and hostile natural conditions, appears to be lost when the 6,000,000 have grown to 70,000,000, and are already reckoning the day when they will be 200,000,000. The people whom Henry Adams described as living at the beginning of the nineteenth century "in an isolation like that of the Jutes and Angles of the fifth century" have tamed a continent, have covered it with a vast network of the most magnificent railroads in the world, have grown to be the largest and most homogeneous nation on the face of the earth, with a great world-movement behind it, and certainly a great world-part in the future before it. It is because the man in the Western states to-day, in a dim instinctive way, realizes these things, because he has himself been in the midst of this development, and has even been a factor in it, that he seems to be willing to take the risks which more theoretical minds hesitate at. That was the answer which I gave myself. To look closer at the matter is only to have the importance of it brought home with increased force.

The struggle above described has been going on ever since, and it is but the last phase of it that we have had in America in the recent war with Spain. Yet the conditions are slowly changing. A leading factor in the future history of the world is that it is the probable distiny of the United States, at no distant time, to become the leading section of the English-speaking world; nay, not only that, but to become the leading world-power of the next century. Now, if the United States is going to be a great world-power in the next century, it would seem to be almost impossible to conceive that it will be able to escape the effect of its connection with what are really world-principles, and these world-principles will involve very important relationships to the world in the future. The first matter with which it will undoubtedly be concerned is the trade of the world.

It is not possible to conceive the North American continent as occupied by perhaps 200,000,000 people in the near future, without considering these inhabitants as having behind them a world-trade. Some persons seem to think that a country may have an export trade without an import trade. It is an economic law that even that is impossible. When we come to look at the world of the present day, it may be seen at once that most of the developments that have gone on in the past have been those which have taken place in the temperate regions. We of the more vigorous races have been occupied during the last century or two with colonizing, spreading ourselves over, and taming the temperate regions of the world. That era, it would seem, will not last much longer; it is slowly but surely coming to a close. Within a time which many of us will live to see, the American continent will be settled up; it is very nearly settled up already, in the agricultural sense. The next era of expansion, which we are almost in the midst of, is the great era of industrial expansion, manufacturing expansion,—an era of expansion which will undoubtedly bring the United States into very important relations with the trade of the world. The people of the United States will be driven to seek the widest possible outside market for their industrial productions; they must be able to buy raw material in outside markets; and they will have behind them, as they will come to realize more and more clearly, a great history, for they will be the leading representatives of definite principles in the development of the world.

Now let us see what this trade means. It would seem that there can be little doubt that the trade of the world in the future will be largely a trade wtih the tropics. The tropics are naturally the most richly endowed portion of the world. Under proper conditions of administration, the possibilities of production in the tropics are immensely greater than the possibilities of production in the temperate regions. Even with the extremely unfavorable conditions which at present prevail in the tropics, as I have elsewhere tried to show, our civilization already rests to a large extent on its trade with the tropics. . . .

If we exclude consideration of trade within the English-speaking regions, the total trade of the United States with the tropics in 1895 was $346,000,000 as against $535,000,000 with the remainder of the world. This is a very striking and pregnant fact when we consider existing conditions. It must always be kept in view, too, that no nation can remain permanently indifferent to the condition of a country with which it has large and vital trade relations. Although the United States interfered in Cuba in the cause of humanity, it must be remembered that it was the close trade connection of the American people with the island which directly and forcibly compelled the attention of the public mind to what was taking place there. For all these reasons, it seems hard to believe that traditions of the past, which opposed a policy of expansion on the part of the United States, will operate with the same force in the future.

For the same reason that expansion appears to the Western man to be inevitable, there is a disposition to regard wtih equanimity the apparently "insuperable practical difficulty to a policy of expansion in the inefficient civil service of the United States." One of the most remarkable, and, if I mistake not, one of the most healthy symptoms of public life in America, is a disposition to regard with a cheerful optimism those problems of government which do so much to depress the English observer. As yet, America probably has not taken seriously in hand the treatment of these problems, and the results will likely enough be striking when the task is earnestly undertaken. The United States is the highest, and yet the youngest, of all political organisms in the world,—an organism with a promise and a potentiality behind it of which there has been no previous parallel; but it has hardly had time to attend to the problems, the slow solution of which has taken hundreds of years in other countries. There seems to be no insurmountable reason why there should not be as efficient a civil service in the United States as there is in England. . . .

As to the question implied in the third proposition I have no right to reply. It is a matter exclusively for the American people. I would point out, however, that in this question the control of *colonies* by the United States is spoken of. One of the leading principles that I have tried to enunciate in my book on the control of the tropics is that such territories can never be *colonies;* that the white man can never be acclimatized in the tropics; that such regions must continue to be permanently peopled by their *natural* inhabitants; and that the highest duty of the civilized power that undertakes responsibility in relation thereto is to see that they shall be governed, not in the interest of the governing power, but as a trust for civilization.

As to the logic of the situation, that is also a matter solely for the American people. Yet it is one of the deepest truths of philosophy that the meaning of living things cannot be put into logical formulas. The spirit behind the Constitution of the United States is probably one of the most vital and healthy things in the world; and yet, under the Constitution itself, there are already the most illogical results. One of the fundamental principles of government in the United States is the assumption of the right of every citizen to liberty and the pursuit of happiness. The negro is a citizen of the United States, and yet in some states of the Union he is is forbidden to marry a citizen of a different color. The Indian is a ward of the United States, and not a citizen; and the Chinaman is forbidden a vote. All this is illogical. But it is not therefore wrong; and the fact remains that the spirit behind the American Constitution is probably one of the healthiest forces in the world. The intense feeling of the Western man that there is a meaning and a reason behind a policy of expansion which cannot be put into formulas—which it is not even necessary to put into formulas—has more in it than appears on the surface; it may be nearer to the real meaning of things than the most thoroughly reasoned argument. We have not had a more philosophical historian in England than Professor Seeley, certainly none who has understood better the meaning of the principles behind the expansion of the English-speaking races. It was he who, writing about such principles, delivered himself of this remarkable saying: "In a truly living institution the instinct of development is wiser than the utterances of the wisest individual man." That is the Western man's conclusion put into the philosophy of the historian.

21 FROM   *Samuel L. Clemens*
To the Person Sitting in Darkness

The real bite in this invective against the civilization trust derives from Mark Twain's inversion of traditional sun symbolism. Yet his major assumption, that we Americans should behave differently from Europeans was, as we have learned, a major premise of Manifest Destiny. Mark Twain's side of the argument helped carry the day for the gradual independence of the Philippines, but did little to stop American intervention elsewhere. The self-denying Teller Amendment to President McKinley's War Resolution against Spain, for instance, which disclaimed any intention to control Cuba after the war, was seriously crippled by a 1901 amendment making Cuba a quasi-protectorate. As a result, the United States still holds within Castro's revolutionary Cuba the gigantic Guantànamo naval base, and some critics blame selfish United States commercial policy for creating the monster that Fidele Castro overthrew. During this postwar period, the United States actively pursued its open door policy in China, intervened in Nicaragua, precipitated a Colombian revolution to ensure control of the projected isthmian canal and, in general, practised "dollar diplomacy" in Latin America, backed by Roosevelt's threat of "the big stick." These activities bred a continuing reputation for the United States—not to be dispelled by United States initiative in arranging arbitration between great powers and promoting disarmament treaties—as "policeman of the world."

Although individual Americans, as has been seen, had predicted and desired such a world role since early colonial days, the great question remains: whether this outcome can be called imperialism and, if so, whether it differs significantly from nine-

SOURCE. Originally sponsored by the Anti-Imperialist League of New York and published in the *North American Review* for February, 1901. Reprinted here from Samuel L. Clemens, *Europe and Elsewhere* (New York: Harper and Brothers, 1923) , pp. 250–272.

teenth-century American ideology and practice. Mark Twain, long a proponent of the self-denying messianic example as opposed to messianic intervention, makes no bones about it. This is imperialism in the old European mold, a situation of which his countrymen seem unaware—and, hence, the savagery of his indictment, depending on an old truism, that Americans seldom do wrong knowingly. The symbolism in his treatment of light and dark people certainly suggests a parallel in the treatment of American Indians.

. . . The following is from the New York *Tribune* of Christmas Eve. It comes from that journal's Tokyo correspondent. It has a strange and impudent sound, but the Japanese are but partially civilized as yet. When they become wholly civilized they will not talk so:

"The missionary question, of course, occupies a foremost place in the discussion. It is now felt as essential that the Western Powers take cognizance of the sentiment here, that religious invasions of Oriental countries by powerful Western organizations are tantamount to filibustering expeditions, and should not only be discountenanced, but that stern measures should be adopted for their suppression. The feeling here is that the missionary organizations constitute a constant menace to peaceful international relations."

Shall we? That is, shall we go on conferring our Civilization upon the peoples that sit in darkness, or shall we give those poor things a rest? Shall we bang right ahead in our old-time, loud, pious way, and commit the new century to the game; or shall we sober up and sit down and think it over first? Would it not be prudent to get our Civilization tools together and see how much stock is left on hand in the way of Glass Beads and Theology, and Maxim Guns and Hymn Books, and Trade Gin and Torches of Progress and Enlightenment (patent adjustable ones, good to fire villages with, upon occasion) , and balance the books and arrive at the profit and loss, so that we may intelligently decide

whether to continue the business or sell out the property and
start a new Civilization Scheme on the proceeds?

Extending the Blessings of Civilization to our Brother who Sits
in Darkness has been a good trade and has paid well, on the
whole; and there is money in it yet, if carefully worked—but not
enough, in my judgment, to make any considerable risk advisable. The People that Sit in Darkness are getting to be too scarce
—too scarce and too shy. And such darkness as is now left is
really of but an indifferent quality, and not dark enough for the
game. The most of those People that Sit in Darkness have been
furnished with more light than was good for them or profitable
for us. We have been injudicious.

The Blessings-of-Civilization Trust, wisely and cautiously administered, is a Daisy. There is more money in it, more territory,
more sovereignty and other kinds of emolument, than there is in
any other game that is played. But Christendom has been playing
it badly of late years and must certainly suffer by it, in my opinion. She has been so eager to get every stake that appeared on
the green cloth that the People who Sit in Darkness have noticed
it—they have noticed it and have begun to show alarm. They
have become suspicious of the Blessings of Civilization. More—
they have begun to examine them. This is not well. The Blessings
of Civilization are all right, and a good commercial property;
there could not be a better, in a dim light. In the right kind of a
light and at a proper distance, with the goods a little out of focus, they furnish this desirable exhibit to the Gentlemen who Sit
in Darkness:

LOVE	LAW AND ORDER
JUSTICE	LIBERTY
GENTLENESS	EQUALITY
CHRISTIANITY	HONORABLE DEAL-
PROTECTION TO THE	ING
WEAK	MERCY
TEMPERANCE	EDUCATION

—and so on.

There. Is it good? Sir, it is pie. It will bring into camp any idi-
ot that sits in darkness anywhere. But not if we adulterate it. It is

proper to be emphatic upon that point. This brand is strictly for Export—apparently. *Apparently*. Privately and confidentially, it is nothing of the kind. Privately and confidentially, it is merely an outside cover, gay and pretty and attractive, displaying the special patterns of our Civilization which we reserve for Home Consumption, while *inside* the bale is the Actual Thing that the Customer Sitting in Darkness buys with his blood and tears and land and liberty. The Actual Thing is indeed Civilization, but it is only for Export. Is there a difference between the two brands? In some of the details, yes.

We all know that the Business is being ruined. The reason is not far to seek. It is because our Mr. McKinley, and Mr. Chamberlain,* and the Kaiser and the Tsar and the French have been exporting the Actual Thing *with the outside cover left off.* This is bad for the Game. It shows that these new players of it are not sufficiently acquainted with it.

It is a distress to look on and note the mismoves, they are so strange and so awkward. Mr. Chamberlain manufactures a war out of materials so inadequate and so fanciful that they make the boxes grieve and the gallery laugh, and he tries hard to persuade himself that it isn't purely a private raid for cash but has a sort of dim, vague respectability about it somewhere, if he could only find the spot; and that by and by he can scour the flag clean again after he has finished dragging it through the mud, and make it shine and flash in the vault of heaven once more as it had shone and flashed there a thousand years in the world's respect until he laid his unfaithful hand upon it. It is bad play— bad. For it exposes the Actual Thing to Them that Sit in Darkness, and they say: "What! Christian against Christian? And only for money? Is *this* a case of magnanimity, forbearance, love, gentleness, mercy, protection of the weak—this strange and overshowy onslaught of an elephant upon a nest of field mice, on the pretext that the mice had squeaked an insolence at him— conduct which 'no self-respecting government could allow to pass unavenged'? as Mr. Chamberlain said. Was that a good pretext in a small case, when it had not been a good pretext in a

---

* Joseph Chamberlain (1836–1914), British imperialistic statesman, was accused of promoting the Boer War of 1899 to 1902 in South Africa.

large one?—for only recently Russia had affronted the elephant three times and survived alive and unsmitten. Is this Civilization and Progress? Is it something better than we already possess? These harryings and burnings and desert-makings in the Transvaal—is this an improvement on our darkness? Is it, perhaps, possible that there are two kinds of Civilization—one for home consumption and one for the heathen market?"

Then They that Sit in Darkness are troubled, and shake their heads, and they read this extract from a letter of a British private, recounting his exploits in one of Methuen's victories some days before the affair of Magersfontein, and they are troubled again:

"We tore up the hill and into the intrenchments, and the Boers saw we had them; so they dropped their guns and went down on their knees and put up their hands clasped, and begged for mercy. And we gave it them—*with the long spoon*."

The long spoon is the bayonet. See *Lloyd's Weekly*, London, of those days. The same number—and the same column—contained some quite unconscious satire in the form of shocked and bitter upbraidings of the Boers for their brutalities and inhumanities!

Next, to our heavy damage, the Kaiser went to playing the game without first mastering it. He lost a couple of missionaries in a riot in Shantung, and in his account he made an overcharge for them. China had to pay a hundred thousand dollars apiece for them in money; twelve miles of territory, containing several millions of inhabitants and worth twenty million dollars; and to build a monument and also a Christian church; whereas the people of China could have been depended upon to remember the missionaries without the help of these expensive memorials. This was all bad play. Bad, because it would not, and could not, and will not now or ever, deceive the Person Sitting in Darkness. He knows that it was an overcharge. He knows that a missionary is like any other man: he is worth merely what you can supply his place for and no more. He is useful, but so is a doctor, so is a sheriff, so is an editor; but a just Emperor does not charge war prices for such. A diligent, intelligent, but obscure missionary, and a diligent, intelligent country editor are worth much, and we know it; but they are not worth the earth. We esteem such an editor and we are sorry to see him go, but when he goes, we should consider twelve miles of territory and a church and a fortune over-compensation for his loss. I mean, if he was a Chinese editor and we had to settle for him. It is no proper figure for an editor or a missionary; one can get shop-worn kings for less. It was bad play on the Kaiser's part. It got this property, true; but it *produced the Chinese revolt,* the indignant uprising of China's traduced patriots, the Boxers. The results have been expensive to Germany and to the other Disseminators of Progress and the Blessings of Civilization.

The Kaiser's claim was paid, yet it was bad play, for it could not fail to have an evil effect upon Persons Sitting in Darkness in China. They would muse upon the event and be likely to say: "Civilization is gracious and beautiful, for such is its reputation, but can we afford it? There are rich Chinamen, perhaps they can afford it; but this tax is not laid upon them, it is laid upon the peasants of Shantung; it is they that must pay this mighty sum and their wages are but four cents a day. Is this a better civilization than ours, and holier and higher and nobler? Is not this rapacity? Is not this extrotion? Would Germany charge America two hundred thousand dollars for two missionaries, and shake the mailed fist in her face and send warships and send soldiers, and say, 'Seize twelve miles of territory, worth twenty millions of dollars, as additional pay for the missionaries, and make those peasants build a monument to the missionaries, and a costly Christian church to remember them by?' And later would Germany say to her soldiers, 'March through America and slay, *giving no quarter;* make the German face there, as has been our Hun-face here, a terror for a thousand years; march through the Great Republic and slay, slay, slay, carving a road for our offended religion through its heart and bowels?' Would Germany do like this to America, to England, to France, to Russia? Or only to China, the helpless—imitating the elephant's assault upon the field mice? Had we better invest in this Civilization— this Civilization which called Napoleon a buccaneer for carrying off Venice's bronze horses, but which steals our ancient astronomical instruments from our walls and goes looting like common bandits—that is, all the alien soldiers except America's; and

(Americans again excepted) storms frightened villages and ca-
bles the result to glad journals at home every day: "Chinese losses, 450 killed; ours, *one officer and two men wounded.* Shall
proceed against neighboring village tomorrow, where a *massacre*
is reported.' Can we afford Civilization?"

And next Russia must go and play the game injudiciously. She
affronts England once or twice—with the Person Sitting in
Darkness observing and noting; by moral assistance of France
and Germany, she robs Japan of her hard-earned spoil, all swimming in Chinese blood—Port Arthur—with the Person again
observing and noting; then she seizes Manchuria, raids its villages, and chokes its great river with the swollen corpses of
countless massacred peasants—that astonished Person still observing and noting. And perhaps he is saying to himself, "It is
yet *another* Civilized Power, with its banner of the Prince of
Peace in one hand and its loot basket and its butcher knife in the
other. Is there no salvation for us but to adopt Civilization and
lift ourselves down to its level?"

And by and by comes America, and our Master of the Game
plays it badly—plays it as Mr. Chamberlain was playing it in
South Africa. It was a mistake to do that; also, it was one which
was quite unlooked for in a Master who was playing it so well in
Cuba. In Cuba, he was playing the usual and regular *American*
game and it was winning, for there is no way to beat it. The
Master, contemplating Cuba, said, "Here is an oppressed and
friendless little nation which is willing to fight to be free; we go
partners, and put up the strength of seventy million sympathizers
and the resources of the United States: play!" Nothing but Europe combined could call that hand, and Europe cannot combine
on anything. There in Cuba he was following our great traditions
in a way which made us very proud of him, and proud of the
deep dissatisfaction which his play was provoking in continental
Europe. Moved by a high inspiration, he threw out those stirring
words which proclaimed that forcible annexation would be
"criminal aggression," and in that utterance fired another "shot
heard round the world." The memory of that fine saying will be
outlived by the remembrance of no act of his but one—that he
forgot it within the twelvemonth, and its honorable gospel along
with it.

For presently came the Philippine temptation. It was strong, it was too strong, and he made that bad mistake: he played the European game, the Chamberlain game. It was a pity, it was a great pity, that error—that one grievous error, that irrevocable error. For it was the very place and time to play the American game again. And at no cost. Rich winnings to be gathered in, too, rich and permanent, indestructible, a fortune transmissible forever to the children of the flag. Not land, not money, not dominion—no, something worth many times more than that dross: our share, the spectacle of a nation of long harassed and persecuted slaves set free through our influence; our posterity's share, the golden memory of that fair deed. The game was in our hands. If it had been played according to the American rules, Dewey would have sailed away from Manila as soon as he had destroyed the Spanish fleet—after putting up a sign on shore guaranteeing foreign property and life against damage by the Filipinos, and warning the Powers that interference with the emancipated patriots would be regarded as an act unfriendly to the United States. The Powers cannot combine in even a bad cause, and the sign would not have been molested.

Dewey could have gone about his affairs elsewhere and left the competent Filipino army to starve out the little Spanish garrison and send it home, and the Filipino citizens to set up the form of government they might prefer and deal with the friars and their doubtful acquisitions according to Filipino ideas of fairness and justice—ideas which have since been tested and found to be of as high an order as any that prevail in Europe or America.

But we played the Chamberlain game and lost the chance to add another Cuba and another honorable deed to our good record.

The more we examine the mistake, the more clearly we perceive that it is going to be bad for the Business. The Person Sitting in Darkness is almost sure to say, "There is something curious about this—curious and unaccountable. There must be two Americas, one that sets the captive free, and one that takes a once-captive's new freedom away from him, and picks a quarrel with him with nothing to found it on, then kills him to get his land."

The truth is, the Person Sitting in Darkness *is* saying things like that, and for the sake of the Business we must persuade him to look at the Philippine matter in another and healthier way. We must arrange his opinions for him. I believe it can be done, for Mr. Chamberlain has arranged England's opinion of the South African matter and done it most cleverly and successfully. He presented the facts—some of the facts—and showed those confiding people what the facts meant. He did it statistically, which is a good way. He used the formula: "Twice 2 are 14, and 2 from 9 leaves 35." Figures are effective; figures will convince the elect.

Now, my plan is a still bolder one than Mr. Chamberlain's, though apparently a copy of it. Let us be franker than Mr. Chamberlain; let us audaciously present the whole of the facts, shirking none, then explain them according to Mr. Chamberlain's formula. This daring truthfulness will astonish and dazzle the Person Sitting in Darkness, and he will take the Explanation down before his mental vision has had time to get back into focus. Let us say to him:

"Our case is simple. On the first of May, Dewey destroyed the Spanish fleet. This left the Archipelago in the hands of its proper and rightful owners, the Filipino nation. Their army numbered 30,000 men and they were competent to whip out or starve out the little Spanish garrison; then the people could set up a government of their own devising. Our traditions required that Dewey should now set up his warning sign and go away. But the Master of the Game happened to think of another plan—the European plan. He acted upon it. This was to send out an army—ostensibly to help the native patriots put the finishing touch upon their long and plucky struggle for independence, but really to take their land away from them and keep it. That is, in the interest of Progress and Civilization. The plan developed stage by stage, and quite satisfactorily. We entered into a military alliance with the trusting Filipinos and they hemmed in Manila on the land side, and by their valuable help the place, with its garrison of 8,000 or 10,000 Spaniards, was captured—a thing which we could not have accomplished unaided at that time. We got their help by—by ingenuity. We knew they were fighting for their independence and that they had been at it for two years. We knew they supposed that we also were fighting in their worthy cause —just as we had helped the Cubans fight for Cuban independence—and we allowed them to go on thinking so. *Until Manila was ours and we could get along without them.* Then we showed our hand. Of course, they were surprised—that was natural, surprised and disappointed, disappointed and grieved. To them it looked un-American, uncharacteristic, foreign to our established traditions. And this was natural, too, for we were only playing the American Game in public—in private it was the European. It was neatly done, very neatly, and it bewildered them. They could not understand it, for we had been so friendly—so affectionate, even—with those simple-minded patriots! We, our own selves, had brought back out of exile their leader, their hero, their hope, their Washington—Aguinaldo; brought him in a warship, in high honor, under the sacred shelter and hospitality of the flag; brought him back and restored him to his people and got their moving and eloquent gratitude for it. Yes, we had been so friendly to them and had heartened them up in so many ways! We had lent them guns and ammunition; advised with them; exchanged pleasant courtesies with them; placed our sick and wounded in their kindly care; intrusted our Spanish prisoners to their humane and honest hands; fought shoulder to shoulder with them against "the common enemy" (our own phrase) ; praised their courage, praised their gallantry, praised their mercifulness, praised theif fine and honorable conduct; borrowed their trenches, borrowed strong positions which they had previously captured from the Spaniards; petted them, lied to them—officially proclaiming that our land and naval forces came to give them their freedom and displace the bad Spanish Government—fooled them, used them until we needed them no longer, then derided the sucked orange and threw it away. We kept the positions which we had beguiled them of, by and by we moved a force forward and overlapped patriot ground—a clever thought, for we needed trouble and this would produce it. A Filipino soldier, crossing the ground, where no one had a right to forbid him, was shot by our sentry. The badgered patriots resented this with arms, without waiting to know whether Aguinaldo, who was absent, would approve or not. Aguinaldo did not approve, but that availed nothing. What we wanted in the interest of Progress and Civilization was the Archipelago, unencumbered by patriots struggling for independence; and War was what we needed. We clinched our opportunity. It is Mr. Chamberlain's case over again—at least in its motive and intention; and we played the game as adroitly as he played it himself."

At this point in our frank statement of fact to the Person Sitting in Darkness, we should throw in a little trade taffy about the Blessings of Civilization—for a change, and for the refreshment of his spirit—then go on with our tale:

"We and the patriots having captured Manila, Spain's ownership of the Archipelago and her sovereignty over it were at an end—obliterated—annihilated—not a rag or shred of either remaining behind. It was then that we conceived the divinely humorous idea of *buying* both of these specters from Spain! [It is quite safe to confess this to the Person Sitting in Darkness, since neither he nor any other sane person will believe it.] In buying those ghosts for twenty millions, we also contracted to take care of the friars and their accumulations. I think we also agreed to propagate leprosy and smallpox, but as to this there is doubt. But it is not important, persons afflicted with the friars do not mind other diseases.

"With our Treaty ratified, Manila subdued, and our Ghosts secured, we had no further use for Aguinaldo and the owners of the Archipelago. We forced a war and we have been hunting America's guest and ally through the woods and swamps ever since."

At this point in the tale, it will be well to boast a little of our war work and our heroisms in the field, so as to make our performance look as fine as England's in South Africa, but I believe it will not be best to emphasize this too much. We must be cautious. Of course, we must read the war telegrams to the Person, in order to keep up our frankness, but we can throw an air of humorousness over them and that will modify their grim eloquence a little, and their rather indiscreet exhibitions of gory exultation. Before reading to him the following display heads of the dispatches of November 18, 1900, it will be well to practice on

them in private first, so as to get the right tang of lightness and
gayety into them:

"ADMINISTRATION WEARY OF
PROTRACTED HOSTILITIES!"

"REAL WAR AHEAD FOR FILIPINO
REBELS!"[1]

"WILL SHOW NO MERCY!"
"KITCHENER'S PLAN ADOPTED!"

Kitchener knows how to handle disagreeable people who are
fighting for their homes and their liberties, and we must let on
that we are merely imitating Kitchener and have no national interest in the matter, further than to get ourselves admired by the
Great Family of Nations, in which august company our Master
of the Game has bought a place for us in the back row.

Of course, we must not venture to ignore our General Mac-
Arthur's reports—oh, why do they keep on printing those em-
barrassing things?—we must drop them trippingly from the
tongue and take the chances:

"During the last ten months our losses have been 268 killed
and 750 wounded; Filipino loss, *three thousand two hundred
and twenty-seven killed,* and 694 wounded."

We must stand ready to grab the Person Sitting in Darkness,
for he will swoon away at this confession, saying, "Good God!
those 'niggers' spare their wounded, and the Americans massacre
theirs!"

We must bring him to and coax him and coddle him, and assure him that the ways of Providence are best and that it would
not become us to find fault with them; and then, to show him
that we are only imitators, not originators, we must read the following passage from the letter of an American soldier lad in the
Philippines to his mother, published in *Public Opinion,* of De-
corah, Iowa, describing the finish of a victorious battle:

---

[1] "Rebels!" Mumble that funny word—don't let the Person catch it distinctly.

"WE NEVER LEFT ONE ALIVE. IF ONE WAS WOUNDED, WE WOULD RUN OUR BAYONETS THROUGH HIM."

Having now laid all the historical facts before the Person Sitting in Darkness, we should bring him to again and explain them to him. We should say to him:

"They look doubtful but in reality they are not. There have been lies, yes, but they were told in a good cause. We have been treacherous, but that was only in order that real good might come out of apparent evil. True, we have crushed a deceived and confiding people; we have turned against the weak and the friendless who trusted us; we have stamped out a just and intelligent and well-ordered republic; we have stabbed an ally in the back and slapped the face of a guest; we have bought a Shadow from an enemy that hadn't it to sell; we have robbed a trusting friend of his land and his liberty; we have invited our clean young men to shoulder a discredited musket and do bandits' work under a flag which bandits have been accustomed to fear, not to follow; we have debauched America's honor and blackened her face before the world; but each detail was for the best. We know this. The Head of every State and Sovereignty in Christendom and 90 per cent of every legislative body in Christendom, including our Congress and our fifty state legislatures, are members not only of the church but also of the Blessings-of-Civilization Trust. This world-girdling accumulation of trained morals, high principles, and justice cannot do an unright thing, an unfair thing, an ungenerous thing, an unclean thing. It knows what it is about. Give yourself no uneasiness; it is all right."

Now then, that will convince the Person. You will see. It will restore the Business. Also, it will elect the Master of the Game to the vacant place in the Trinity of our national gods, and there on their high thrones the Three will sit, age after age, in the people's sight, each bearing the Emblem of his service: Washington, the Sword of the Liberator; Lincoln, the Slave's Broken Chains; the Master, the Chains Repaired.

It will give the Business a splendid new start. You will see.

Everything is prosperous, now; everything is just as we should wish it. We have got the Archipelago, and we shall never give it up. Also, we have every reason to hope that we shall have an opportunity before very long to slip out of our congressional contract with Cuba and give her something better in the place of it. It is a rich country and many of us are already beginning to see that the contract was a sentimental mistake. But now—right now —is the best time to do some profitable rehabilitating work— work that will set us up and make us comfortable, and discourage gossip. We cannot conceal from ourselves that, privately, we are a little troubled about our uniform. It is one of our prides, it is acquainted with honor, it is familiar with great deeds and noble, we love it, we revere it, and so this errand it is on makes us uneasy. And our flag—another pride of ours, our chiefest! We have worshiped it so, and when we have seen it in far lands— glimpsing it unexpectedly in that strange sky, waving its welcome and benediction to us—we have caught our breaths and uncovered our heads and couldn't speak for a moment, for the thought of what it was to us and the great ideals it stood for. Indeed, we *must* do something about these things; it is easily managed. We can have a special one—our states do it: we can have just our usual flag, with the white stripes painted black and the stars replaced by the skull and crossbones.

And we do not need that Civil Commission out there. Having no powers, it has to invent them, and that kind of work cannot be effectively done by just anybody; an expert is required. Mr. Croker can be spared. We do not want the United States represented there, but only the Game.

By help of these suggested amendments, Progress and Civilization in that country can have a boom, and it will take in the Persons who are sitting in Darkness, and we can resume Business at the old stand.

PART FIVE

The American Century

QUOTABLE QUOTES

"This is a fight between a slave world and a free world. Just as the United States in 1862 could not remain half slave and half free, so in 1942 the world must make its decision for a complete victory one way or the other. . . . Some have spoken of the "American Century." I say that the century on which we are entering—the century which will come out of this war—can be and must be the century of the common man. Perhaps it will be America's opportunity to suggest the freedoms and duties by which the common man must live."

Henry A. Wallace, 1942

"Many argue that an Atlantic axis is natural and necessary, but maintain, in effect, that Kipling was right, and that the Asian peoples are so "different" that Asia itself is only peripherally an American concern. . . . At the same time, the fact that the United States has now fought three Asian wars in the space of a generation is grimly but truly symbolic of the deepening involvement of the United States in what happens on the other side of the Pacific. . . . The United States is a Pacific power. Europe has been withdrawing the remnants of empire, but the United States, with its coast reaching in an arc from Mexico to the Bering Straits, is one anchor of a vast Pacific community. Both our interests and our ideals propel us westward across the Pacific, not as conquerors but as partners. . . ."

Richard M. Nixon, 1967

"It may be hard for the world to realize it, but there is one nation that the good Lord has put upon the earth which seems to have the resources, material and spiritual, to wish to secure for mankind the rule of law and justice. It may be hard to get the world to accept that as a reality, but we must try."

Jacob Javits, 1966

"If we wish to encourage the spread of democracy and freedom, primary reliance must be on the force of our example: on the qualities of the societies we build in our own countries—what we stand for at home and abroad."

Robert Kennedy, 1965

"COMMAGER DECLARES U. S. OVEREXTENDS WORLD ROLE"

"The United States, he said, must learn that there are limitations and restraints on the applications of its 'immense power.' Such restraints, he suggested, are in keeping with the American tradition of limitations on the power of the Government.

"But he argued that these traditional principles had been overcome by a 'moralistic obsession' with stopping Communism and a 'messianic' feeling that the United States had a 'deep obligation' to advance and spread democracy throughout the world.

Dr. Henry Steele Commager
before the Senate Foreign Relations
Committee as reported by
The New York Times *for February 21,*
1967.

22 FROM *Henry Luce*
The American Century

As founder-editor of Life *and* Time *magazines with reader circulation in the millions, rivaled only by* Reader's Digest, *Luce, the son of China missionaries, was the chief carrier of Manifest Destiny into the mid-twentieth century—long after historians had supposedly buried this doctrine in ceremonious footnotes. The present reader must judge for himself whether Manifest Destiny has acquired a new life in the selection below. One critic of this same article (in the* Nation *for November 2, 1957, pp. 297–301) thought that the orbit of Sputnik I gave the lie to its message. For a startling similar statement which has been called "one of the great statements of the war aims of the United Nations," consult Henry A. Wallace, "The Price of a Free World Victory," as reprinted in Thorp, Curti, and Baker, editors,* American Issues, Volume One: The Social Record *(Copyright, 1944, by J. B. Lippincott Company), pp. 1036–1041.*

In general, the issues which the American people champion revolve around their determination to make the society of men

SOURCE. Henry R. Luce, "The American Century," *Life* (February 17, 1941) , p. 65.

safe for the freedom, growth and increasing satisfaction of all individual men. Beside that resolve, the sneers, groans, catcalls,
teeth-grinding, hisses and roars of the Nazi Propaganda Ministry
are of small moment.

Once we cease to distract ourselves with lifeless arguments
about isolationism, we shall be amazed to discover that there is
already an immense American internationalism. American jazz,
Hollywood movies, American slang, American machines and
patented products, are in fact the only things that every community in the world, from Zanzibar to Hamburg, recognizes in
common. Blindly, unintentionally, accidentally and really in spite
of ourselves, we are already a world power in all the trivial ways
—in very human ways. But there is a great deal more than that.
America is already the intellectual, scientific and artistic capital
of the world. Americans—Midwestern Americans—are today
the least provincial people in the world. They have traveled the
most and they know more about the world than the people of
any other country. America's worldwide experience in commerce
is also far greater than most of us realize.

Most important of all, we have that indefinable, unmistakable
sign of leadership: prestige. And unlike the prestige of Rome or
Genghis Khan or 19th Century England, American prestige
throughout the world is faith in the good intentions as well as in
the ultimate intelligence and ultimate strength of the whole
American people. We have lost some of that prestige in the last
few years. But most of it is still there.

* * *

No narrow definition can be given to the American internationalism of the 20th Century. It will take shape, as all civilizations take shape, by the living of it, by work and effort, by trial
and error, by enterprise and adventure and experience.

And by imagination!

As America enters dynamically upon the world scene, we
need most of all to seek and to bring forth a vision of America as
a world power which is authentically American and which can
inspire us to live and work and fight with vigor and enthusiasm.
And as we come now to the great test, it may yet turn out that in
all our trials and tribulations of spirit during the first part of this

century we as a people have been painfully apprehending the meaning of our time and now in this moment of testing there may come clear at last the vision which will guide us to the authentic creation of the 20th Century—our Century.

* * *

Consider four areas of life and thought in which we may seek to realize such a vision:

First, the economic. It is for America and for America alone to determine whether a system of free economic enterprise—an economic order compatible with freedom and progress—shall or shall not prevail in this century. We know perfectly well that there is not the slightest chance of anything faintly resembling a free economic system prevailing in this country if it prevails nowhere else. What then does America have to decide? Some few decisions are quite simple. For example: we have to decide whether or not we shall have for ourselves and our friends freedom of the seas—the right to go with our ships and our ocean-going airplanes where we wish, when we wish and as we wish. The vision of America as the principal guarantor of the freedom of the seas, the vision of Americas as the dynamic leader of world trade, has within it the possibilities of such enormous human progress as to stagger the imagination. Let us not be staggered by it. Let us rise to its tremendous possibilities. Our thinking of world trade today is on ridiculously small terms. For example, we think of Asia as being worth only a few hundred millions a year to us. Actually, in the decades to come Asia will be worth to us exactly zero—or else it will be worth to us four, five, ten billions of dollars a year. And the latter are the terms we must think in, or else confess a pitiful impotence.

Closely akin to the purely economic area and yet quite different from it, there is the picture of an America which will send out through the world its technical and artistic skills. Engineers, scientists, doctors, movie men, makers of entertainment, developers of airlines, builders of roads, teachrs, eduactors. Throughout the world, these skills, this training, this leadership is needed and will be eagerly welcomed, if only we have the imagination to see it and the sincerity and good will to create the world of the 20th Century.

But now there is a third thing which our vision must immediately be concerned with. We must undertake now to be the Good Samaritan of the entire world. It is the manifest duty of this country to undertake to feed all the people of the world who as a result of this worldwide collapse of civilization are hungry and destitute—all of them, that is, whom we can from time to time reach consistently with a very tough attitude toward all hostile governments. For every dollar we spend on armaments, we should spend at least a dime in a gigantic effort to feed the world —and all the world should know that we have dedicated ourselves to this task. Every farmer in America should be encouraged to produce all the crops he can, and all that we cannot eat —and perhaps some of us could eat less—should forthwith be dispatched to the four quarters of the globe as a free gift, administered by a humanitarian army of Americans, to every man, woman and child on this earth who is really hungry.

But all this is not enough. All this will fail and none of it will happen unless our vision of America as a world power includes a passionate devotion to great American ideals. We have some things in this country which are infinitely precious and especially American—a love of freedom, a feeling for the equality of opportunity, a tradition of self-reliance and independence and also of co-operation. In addition to ideals and notions which are especially American, we are the inheritors of all the great principles of Western civilization—above all Justice, the love of Truth, the ideal of Charity. The other day Herbert Hoover said that America was fast becoming the sanctuary of the ideals of civilization. For the moment it may be enough to be the sanctuary of these ideals. But not for long. It now becomes our time to be the powerhouse from which the ideals spread throughout the world and do their mysterious work of lifting the life of mankind from the level of the beasts to what the Psalmist called a little lower than the angels.

America as the dynamic center of ever-widening spheres of enterprise, America as the training center of the skillful servants of mankind, America as the Good Samaritan, really believing again that it is more blessed to give than to receive, and America as the powerhouse of the ideals of Freedom and Justice—out of these elements surely can be fashioned a vision of the 20th

Century to which we can and will devote ourselves in joy and gladness and vigor and enthusiasm.

Other nations can survive simply because they have endured so long—sometimes with more and sometimes with less significance. But this nation, conceived in adventure and dedicated to the progress of man—this nation cannot truly endure unless there courses strongly through its veins from Maine to California the blood of purposes and enterprise and high resolve.

Throughout the 17th Century and the 18th Century and the 19th Century, this continent teemed with manifold projects and magnificent purposes. Above them all and weaving them all together into the most exciting flag of all the world and of all history was the triumphal purpose of freedom.

It is in this spirit that all of us are called, each to his own measure of capacity, and each in the widest horizon of his vision, to create the first great American Century.

23 FROM *Virgil Jordan*
A House Divided Against Itself

Jordan was at the time of this Lincoln Day address in 1946 president of the powerful lobbying organization, the National Industrial Conference Board, a brain trust of the National Association of Manufacturers. Delivered at Philadelphia's select Union League before a distinguished audience of 500 Republicans, including leading industrialists, his address is sometimes considered the opening gun of the cold war. It came shortly after Winston Churchill's famous "Iron Curtain" address at Fulton, Missouri, to which it refers, and it anticipated, in many respects, the policy of containment formulated by State Department expert, George Kennan, under President Truman and translated later into "massive retaliation" by Secretary of State John Foster Dulles under President Eisenhower.

President Truman's address on Foreign Economic Policy at

SOURCE. Virgil Jordan, "A House Divided Against Itself. . . ," *Vital Speeches of the Day,* XII, No. 14 (May 1, 1946) , 428–433, *passim.*

Baylor University in 1947, although it also identified free institutions with an enlightened international capitalism stamped "U. S. A." as did Jordan, avoided the kind of rhetoric that expressed popular emotional support for cold war policy which Jordan voiced here. Is Jordan's the old rhetoric of Manifest Destiny in a dangerously new global setting?

. . . I think one can pay no better tribute to the memory and ideals of the great American we call "Honest Abe" than to try to be as honest with ourselves, and to recognize that the fundamental struggle to which he gave his life faces us still and again in our time, but now magnified to global dimensions, and puts to the American people as a whole essentially the same kind of challenge of conviction, candor and courage as confronted Lincoln and the Federal Government in the Civil War. All that I propose to attempt tonight is to explain why I think this is so, and to suggest how we might rise to that challenge in the issue that faces us today.

To do this I must turn back, not six years to my funny prophecies about foreign affairs in 1940, but twelve years, to the last time I had the privilege of speaking to The Union League, in April, 1934, when I tried the patience, and I think the credulity, of my audience by interpreting some of the implications of the New Deal program. . . . We know now that it was naïve to suppose that anything essential in that New Deal revolution was indigenous, native or natural to the mind or morals of America, no matter what the emergency of depression that then disguised or excused it. As we witness its outcome today we recognize at last that it was as much and as fundamentally a foreign invasion as though, six years later, an army of Nazi soldiers, administrators and economists, or Soviet Commissars, had landed in Chesapeake Bay and occupied the capital, or taken forty-two square miles in Connecticut.

Every essential economic idea and moral principle which it applied and implied was imported from Europe or Asia, profoundly alien to the spirit, purpose and experience of the American people, even as long ago as 1933, though perhaps or apparently not so much so today. The doctrines of the disappearance of the frontier, of the onset of economic maturity, of over-saving, of government spending, deficit financing, compensatory fiscal policy, the mixed economy and of government control and economic planning—to mention some of the successive slogans and semantic catchwords of the New Deal—all these are the Dead Sea fruit of the fatalism and despair of the Old World, with which its academic and political dope-peddlers have drugged and bewildered the American people during that decade, until the emotional unity and the economic stimulus of the war's crusade saved them, and the New Deal itself, from the economic and moral bankruptcy which seemed to be the inescapable outcome of the waste, confusion, conflict and stagnation it produced. Whatever may have prepared the way for it before, this decade of the New Deal which imported the old delusion of ominpotent government into the mind and spirit of the American people divided them in understanding and aspiration more deeply than anything in their history had before, and the cleavage it produced aligned them unconsciously but inevitably thereafter with the fantasies, futilities, and fatalities of the class struggles of the Old World.

So it is that having emerged from this war for world freedom without winning it or even ending it, we are living today by an economic organization and under political principles which are in nearly all essentials the same as those that have impoverished, wasted and destroyed the Old World beyond hope of redemption; with a government of unlimited power determining wages, prices, profits, production, employment, consumption, investment, management and ownership of property, for today and the indefinite future, practically by personal decree, or according to some plan or purpose whose meaning is beyond our comprehension and the responsibility for which has passed beyond our control. Many Americans who have the living memory of freedom in their minds fear or hate these things as falsehood or tyranny, but many others who have long forgotten, if they ever knew it in the alien climate which once shaped their spirits, hail them with hope or support them with passion as the promise of prosperity and security to come; and in the eroded soil of dissension and misunderstanding that fills this chasm in our American consciousness, the dragon seed of domestic and international conflict is being sown and our power at home and abroad is being weakened and dissipated by those who expect to profit thereby.

The fact that so many in America have accepted the superstition of omnipotent government and become dependent upon its apparatus during the past decade which culminated in the war means much more than an idle drift down the tides of mass ignorance, indifference or indolence on which the traditional demagogue of the Old World or the new has so often floated his craft and fished in troubled waters. In our time and in this place it is the most important expression of a deliberate, carefully designed and continuously directed world-wide conspiracy to capture and maintain permanent political power over the masses of men everywhere, by crippling, paralyzing and capturing for its purpose the sole remaining source and center of that power, which rests today in the prodigious productive power of a free America. The evidences of its operation and purpose, and the manifestations of its methods and instruments must be obvious enough to all but its victims, and I shall not elaborate upon them tonight; but to be unable to believe that it exists, or to ignore it in any aspect of domestic conditions or foreign policy, seems to me a sign of extreme innocence or profound anesthesia. Its technique today employs on a planetary scale all the subtle arts and stratagems of trickery and terrorism practiced on the Steppes of Asia for centuries past; but its purpose has no precedent or parallel in history. It is not merely to make sure that the ideas and ideals of the Old World shall reoccupy and conquer America; but to prevent those of America, and the power they imply, from liberating the Old World from its bondage; for those who seek to rule it today know that they can do so only if they can make and keep America economically and morally impotent at this historic moment, when the secret of atomic energy both as productive agent and a political weapon rests in her hands, and as she prepares and hopes to release for the purposes of peace, plenty and freedom the collossal power which she acquired through the war. . . .

I think we must realize by now that totalitarian—and that today means only Communist—imperialism has conquered Europe and Asia even more completely than the Nazi and Jap armies did. It is not merely that the Soviet legions have overrun the Balkans and the Baltic countries and turned out the lights of an entire continent from Calais to Korea, and from the Arctic to the Adriatic, but that in most of the rest of Europe, in Italy, and France, and England, no Red armies were needed to destroy economic freedom and civil liberty. It had been done for them long before by the politicians, businessmen and labor unions of these countries. Though we did not know it, and could not be told it in the early days of the Great Crusade, our armies abroad were fighting for ideas—for a philosophy of life and a conception of government—which, in fact, were dead nearly everywhere in the Old World long before the war began.

What is more important is that all of the ideas for the postwar world which are accepted today in Europe, especially in England and Russia, assume it as an imperative condition for their success that this country be brought within the same system permanently, and every device for shaping American thought and feeling to this end is being used today, as they have been during the past decade. The European and Asiatic statesmen who are planning and building their postwar world on the foundation ideas of National Socialism with a façade of new names, having destroyed the Nazi military power with our aid, know better or sooner than the Nazis did that the world cannot live for long half under socialist serfdom and half under economic freedom. This recognition is no less urgent in the long run for Uncle Joe's totalitarian autarchy than it is for a nation under parliamentary government like England, who must live by trade or starve, and who knows that her postwar planned economy cannot compete in any free markets of the world with the productive power of a free America.

So I say to you that the character of American political institutions and her economic system after this war have become as much a crucial concern of the rest of the world as those of Germany were at its beginning, or as those of Russia were after the last war, but this time in reverse fashion, because in a postwar world of socialist states the idea of economic freedom must remain a subversive revolutionary force internationally as well as internally, just as Bolshevism was after the last war. This fact,

Gentlemen, will furnish the key to most problems of international relations as well as those of domestic policy for another decade or two. . . . Isolation has become as impossible in our time for totalitarian socialism or compulsory collectivism as it is for free competitive capitalism. The brutal fact is that the war left us facing an encircling world of beggars or robbers, whom it has bankrupted of spiritual and material resources for peaceful, self-supporting life henceforth. The global organization in which they pretend to have banded together to safeguard peace and freedom was busted before it began, and today it has plainly become an elaborate apparatus for the purposes either of international parasitism or collectivist conspiracy, or both. To imagine this country surrendering any sort of sovereignty to any kind of world government based upon this or any other organization of nations like it, under current conditions, in view of their character and purposes, and in face of the actual economic and military resources which we command, is an idea which can be the product only of stupidity or treachery. It could be proposed only by men who are either very blind or very dumb, or who are ambassadors of brazen banditry.

"You know, and I know," and all the world knows today, that UNO is morally and economically insolvent. It has not only evaded the vital issue of disarmament; that was ruled out at the start, except for the conquered countries; it has evaded even the issue of exercise of any effective form of police power to preserve the peace, and it has actually become an instrument for promoting internal revolt and external conflict among its members. . . . If we do not make the fullest use of our resources for the purposes of peace and plenty, the internal dissension, confusion and conflict upon which the collectivist virus feeds, and which are being fostered among us with feverish speed, will spread and increasingly cripple and paralyze our power and finally destroy us. In the kind of world in which we live today, Gentlemen, it is profoundly true that the kind of power America commands is a power that must be used to the purposes of peace and freedom from which it sprang or it must perish. It is a dynamic force which must unfold itself to the end of its destiny or die.

Now there is pathos as well as pride in the patent fact that the American people have neither the temperament, impulse nor the talent for any form of imperialism. It is something irrelevant and meaningless in the American climate. Whenever in their history they have been drawn or driven—sometimes by the devices or accidents of domestic conditions—into an imperial struggle in the rest of the world, they have done the job of ending it for the day and then have always abandoned it and gone back to their own. There has never been anything the rest of the world could give them as good as what they have gotten for themselves here at home; there is nothing they have wanted from it except to be let alone. And this is still true; but this war was the last in which they will ever be able to feel that way. The decision they face to-day is, I submit, fundamentally different from any they have had to make in the past, for this time the world cannot and will not let them alone. They have conquered it in fact; they will now be forced to subdue it in spirit and practice to their purpose of peace and freedom or it will destroy them. If anyone complains that the dilemma implies or drives us to a type of imperialism which must end as all others have ended, though its purpose be different, let them make the most of it, for this time we have no other choice, and will not have that one much longer unless we make it now. We must ask the world that surrounds us not merely to accept our power, but to accept our purpose of peace and freedom for our own sake as well as its own, and use it to that end.

Let us, under whatever name you may impute to it, make the only choice we can make and proceed to the inescapable task before us swiftly and in the full confidence that at this crucial moment we still command the power to implement and complete it. Let us without delay have an end to compromise, appeasement and retreat, and dare to repudiate all that has been done to that end and in that name. Let us stop the erosion of our economic and material and moral resources at home and abroad in the hopeless struggle against the pervasive conspiracy to sterilize and waste them. Let us offer them freely to the world for a price that is worthy of our power and our purpose. Let us refuse them to anyone who is using them, as every other nation is today, for any other purpose. Let us demand that whatever else the United Nations Organization may do, it must deal with the essential issue of disarmament without further delay or evasion. If we believe, as many in America and England do, that UNO is not and cannot be the kind of international instrument to which the police power of maintaining world peace can safely be entrusted, let us face the fact ourselves and confront the world with it frankly and fearlessly. If we should find that England has so far slipped or been shoved down the slope of collectivist impotence, or is so hopelessly crippled by the problems of her imperialism that she is unwilling or unable to make more than a sleeping partnership with us in the enterprise, let us prepare to undertake the task of policing the world for peace ourselves alone, till—and I doubt it would be very long—we enlist other willing volunteers. Let us then alone or together implement the purpose promptly and plainly in three specific ways:

Let us first offer the utmost capacity of our economic power for reconstruction to every people who will undertake to abolish all national military expenditure and disarm down to the level of the local constabulary. Let us, secondly, demand the unlimited right of continuous inspection and control of every industrial operation and process or every public policy which may have the most remote relationship to armament and warfare. And, finally, let us make, keep and improve our atomic bombs for this imperative purpose; let us suspend them in principle over every place in the world where we have any reason to suspect evasion or conspiracy against this purpose; and let us drop them in fact, promptly and without compunction wherever it is defied.

Now if you say, Gentlemen, that this is too daring or idealistic a destiny for any nation, even America, to embrace, I admit it could happen only once in history; for the dreadful fact is that only we could do it at all or ever; and we can do it only now, today, if we have the understanding and the will. Everything else the American people have—impartiality and purity of moral purpose, limitless potentials of economic power will be realized only if we are willing to employ them for this purpose. . . .

24   FROM   *Denna Frank Fleming*
Manifest Destiny in Vietnam

In this final selection, Denna Frank Fleming, Professor Emeritus of International Relations at Vanderbilt University, journalist, and author, best known for his two-volume study, The Cold War and its Origins *(Garden City, New York, 1961), traces important connections between Manifest Destiny and American involvement in the Vietnam War. He also recapitulates many of the themes expressed in earlier documents in this book. Hence, our volume closes appropriately with a long backward look from a contemporary perspective.*

It is a perspective loosely associated with a "New Left" school of interpretation that has had little doubt about the imperialistic nature of United States expansion and that stands in sharp contrast to the frequent disclaimers of imperialism by Manifest Destiny ideologues and historians. Analysis in this document suggests that critics have been talking about a new kind of imperialism such as that advocated in Document 20 by Benjamin Kidd which does not require colonies, military occupation, or overt political subjection to be operative.

The Cold War is twenty years old and it is obviously waning in its main theater. During World War II Roosevelt and Hull labored long to create a basis for making and keeping the peace in cooperation with the Soviet Union, the great ally which had borne the heavy brunt of the fighting on land and suffered most from death and destruction. However, when Roosevelt and Hull passed from the scene in 1945 their successors abruptly reversed their policies and opted for conflict with the Soviet Union over

SOURCE. D. F. Fleming, *America's Role in Asia* (New York: Funk and Wagnalls, 1969), 3–5, 99–105, 139–145.

East Europe, and for the containment and encirclement of both the Soviets and Communism throughout the world.

The same complete reversal of healing policies had happened twice before in our history, after the death of Lincoln and after the fall of Wilson. In 1918 the tragic results of the reversal were delayed, but they came inexorably. The stupidities and agonies and infinite wastes of World War I had convinced many millions of the best citizens the world over that a new start had to be made, a league of nations must be created that would get all the nations into one body and prevent any more suicidal balance-of-power wars between rival alliances. Never in all human history had an overpowering need been so clear and clamant, yet it was quickly denied in the United States Senate, where the opponents of Woodrow Wilson preferred to return to isolation and let the world drift as before. Our lead in refusing responsibility for the peace was followed by Britain and France in the crises of the League of Nations, and the world drifted into a far worse world war in 1939.

We do not know that our leadership in the League of Nations would have made the difference, but we do know that we did not try to make it succeed, except futilely on the fringes of the League during the Manchurian crisis in 1931–1932. In 1945 we dutifully created another league of nations and entered it, but we also plunged at once into two crusades—an old-fashioned balance-of-power fight with the Soviet Union and a crusade against Communism everywhere. In other words, we heavily overcompensated for the failure of isolationism by coming close to assuming responsibility for everything everywhere in the world.

Our quick assumption of global responsibility was signaled by Churchill's iron curtain speech at Fulton, Missouri, in March 1946, in Truman's applauding presence, and by the proclamation a year later of the Truman Doctrine, forbidding the expansion of Communism anywhere and in effect forbidding all revolutions around the globe, since they might turn Communist.

The Truman Doctrine was the rashest and most sweeping commitment ever . made by any government at any time. . . . American foreign policy in East Asia is a disastrous mixture of anti-Communist ideology, containing China as a great power; smashing guerrilla war, once and for all; economic imperialism; belief in our duty to police the world and in our invincible power; step-by-step involvement; and, finally, blind leadership. It must always be remembered, also, that all of these drives have behind them a vast military-industrial complex, ready at all times to supply the power and to profit from the successive wars of *Pax Americana*.

MANIFEST DESTINY

Throughout our history we have faced west with great confidence. Beginning as colonials on our eastern seaboard in the early sixteen hundreds, we gradually subdued the mid-continent and took it from the Indians and the Mexicans. It was our Manifest Destiny, our leaders told us, and all believed it. Arriving at the Pacific Ocean we acquired Alaska and Hawaii and seized the Philippines from Spain.

Toward Europe we had an inferiority complex. We had fled from her shores, in great numbers, down to World War I, but we faced west with full confidence, so much so that the Texas frontiersman who now occupies the White House can rationalize his terrible predicament in Vietnam by talking expansively of our mission in Asia, even proposing to bring the Great Society to Asia, while it is withering at home.

Of course our Manifest Destiny is another term for American imperialism. A long-time friend of the United States, Sir Denis Brogan, accepted us as "the new imperial power" in a recent series of lectures. He did not discuss the powerful expansive forces generated by our dynamic economy, with immense profits constantly demanding investment and reinvestment, but he did find a great deal of our activity abroad to be "innocently imperialist in the sense that it does expect the world to turn American."

He warned also against our pre-Vietnam assumption of our omnipotence, saying: "The world cannot be made, by any exercise of American wisdom or power, a safe and agreeable place to live in. . . . There are many problems in the world which the American people did not create and cannot solve." He cautioned, too, that "the leaders of the new countries cannot be conjured out of the earth by the most massive doses of military aid or straight economic aid."

Pax Americana

Nevertheless, there can be no doubt that, until recently at least, our leaders felt it to be their duty to police the world, certainly the "free world."

All possible doubt about the determination of the Johnson Administration to suppress any violent outbreak of social discontent anywhere in the "free world" was removed by the Pentagon's current proposal to build a fleet of thirty FDLS—"fast deployment logistic ships." Each would be filled with heavy military equipment for two divisions—helicopters, trucks, mobile guns, etc.—to be stationed in harbors or cruising around the world, ready to dash to any "trouble spot" to meet the C-5A jumbo jet transport planes that will be ready in two years to carry seven hundred American troops each and rain them down wherever discontent raises its head.

Fortunately, that impeccable conservative, Senator Richard B. Russell, chairman of the Senate Armed Services Committee, has blocked this fully revealing proposal, for the time being, telling the Senate on March 21, 1967, that "we should not unilaterally assume the function of policing the world. If it is easy to go anywhere and do anything, we will always be going somewhere and doing something." Nothing could be more painfully evident, but Senator Russell's time in the Senate is short and the Pentagon, from McNamara on down, is determined to press the proposal in succeeding Congresses. Only a national rising of disillusioned citizens can really block this final preparation to forbid forever all revolution in the "free world," lest it turn Red or expropriate our properties.

Since the vast underdeveloped world will seethe increasingly as its social problems grow more acute and since other peoples will continue to assert their right to settle their own problems, nothing but a national decision to turn off the Imperial Way can avert a long series of Vietnams. . . .

RED MONOLITH

The American attempt to contain and confine the most numerous and perhaps the most gifted people on earth was grounded originally in the belief that the entire Communist world was a giant monolith, commanded and directed by a superbrain in Moscow. This was never true, but the idea persisted even after the death of Stalin, early in 1953, and long after the rapid splitting apart of Russia and China was evident. Long after the separate evolution of Communism in each East European Communist state was manifest, beginning with Yugoslavia in 1948, our leaders continued to talk of "the Communist conspiracy." As late as January–February 1966 Mr. Rusk was talking about "the Communists" and "their world revolution."

It became constantly clearer that the law of social evolution is inexorable and that it works relentlessly in both communist and capitalist countries, yet we clung to the myth of the Red Monolith. This was because there was continuing fear of communist power and because the communist abolition of private profits was regarded as the ultimate sin which must be eternally fought, since any extension of Communism contracted the area in which private profits could be freely earned.

VIETNAM

It followed that after world War II the people of Vietnam could not be permitted to win their war of independence from France, because they had Communist leaders. We therefore poured nearly $3 billion worth of military and economic aid for France into Vietnam, and Secretary of State Dulles did all that one utterly determined man could do to prevent France from making peace. When he failed he refused to accept the Geneva settlement of 1954, which divided Vietnam purely for the temporary purpose of liquidating the war, and our government worked to make the division permanent.

This had three effects: (1) it frustrated independence for the

South Vietnamese; (2) it reimposed a feudalistic social system on the South Vietnamese peasants, involving the restoration of hated landlord rule; and (3) our Mandarin tyrant Diem plunged the country into bitter and widespread revolt.

After his fall, other alleged "governments" in Saigon failed and in desperation President Johnson began the bombing of North Vietnam of February 7, 1965, alleging that the whole trouble was due to North Vietnamese "aggression." It was claimed that the trickle of aid in men and supplies coming to the aid of the rebels in South Vietnam constituted aggression against the separate nation of South Vietnam by the Vietnamese of the North. A civil war in the South, for which we were responsible, was alleged to be a case of international aggression.

This is the great myth under which the tragedy of Vietnam grinds on. There is no nation in South Vietnam, either legally or actually. There are the old possessing classes, the seven hundred thousand Catholic refugees from North Vietnam who came south after 1954, liberal patriots in the cities who want a new order, and the peasant majority which wants no more tyranny from Saigon. Certainly the bulk of the people want Vietnamese independence and liberation from the corrupt and reactionary South Vietnamese Army, which fights so little and deserts so freely. It is highly significant that only one officer in this army above the rank of lieutenant colonel did not fight on the side of the French during the war of independence. All the others did, including General Ky, and to the Vietnamese nationalists they are all traitors, doubly so because they now fight with us. . . . Our urge to have profitable dealings with Asia is very deep. It led Columbus to discover America and our colonial forefathers to send the famous clipper sailing ships to China. It led John Quincy Adams, who acquired our first foothold on the Pacific in 1819, to celebrate the event as his greatest achievement and William Henry Seward to call the Pacific "the chief theater of events in the world's great hereafter," well before he obtained Alaska for us in 1869.

Walter LaFeber has shown that as early as 1778 a South Carolina historian thought we had laid the foundations of a new empire, which ever moved from east to west, and would enable us to have "our turn to figure on the face of the earth and in the annals of the world." He finds, too, that the long, twenty-five year depression in our industrial centers which began in 1873 led succeeding administrations after 1893 to prefer joining in the struggle for Asian markets to reform of the economy. The annexation of the Philippines in 1898, over the armed resistance of the Filipinos, was a part of this process.

This event came during a long, sustained drive by our churches to Christianize China. Legions of missionaries were sent to save the souls of the Chinese, who often regarded them as a part of the process of Western invasion and control, which lasted more than a century and was only ended by the coming of the Communists to power after World War II.

The vast Chinese cultural and political area, which had demonstrated remarkable continuity for thousands of years, had been subjected to every kind of attack, invasion, occupation and humiliation by the Europeans, who too often treated the natives as dirt. This would have festered long in the soul of any people, but the injury was deepened by the fact that China had immemorially considered herself the center of the universe, beyond which all was barbaric and inferior. John King Fairbank has explained vividly how modernization was an exhilarating process for us— always expanding, conquering and prevailing—but it *destroyed* the old China and degraded her people in the process. He is sure that when Mao speaks of imperialism he thinks mainly of the Western invasions.

Mao cannot forget how the Westerners forced their way into the celestial kingdom, waged wars to enforce subservience, built great alien cities in China's ports, policed her rivers with their gunboats, collected her customs duties and broke down an ancient, viable way of life. Above all, a great and tenacious culture was violated. It does not help us in Chinese minds, either, that we Americans used little force upon China, leaving that to others while under the Open Door doctrine we successfully insisted on obtaining all privileges in China which had been extorted by others.

On our side we are aggrieved that our great missionary effort in China has been so largely negated, and that the great ally across the Pacific which we so wholeheartedly sought to establish after World War II should suddenly became Communist and hostile. We do not understand that Communist China is the real reply to the century of China's trampling by the West, and we greatly resent that this upstart regime forced us to accept a stalemate in the Korean War.

This is one of the main reasons for our clinging to and expanding the close military encirclement of China, which in turn infuriates patriotic Chinese and convinces them that America is their main and implacable enemy, though the current Maoists appear to regard the Soviet Union as their chief foe. . . .

Therefore it would seem to be imperative common sense for us to begin to relax, gradually but steadily, our close encirclement of China, along with our total trade embargo. This hostile embrace was originally due to the accident of World War II leaving us in control of South Korea, Japan, Okinawa, and Formosa. Now we have completed the iron ring by seizing South Vietnam and arming Thailand heavily. . . .

A BIBLIOGRAPHICAL ESSAY

The raw materials of Manifest Destiny as an ideology include Fourth of July orations and other public addresses, speeches in Congress, state papers and memoranda, newspaper editorials, tracts and broadsides, political diaries, travel journals, promotional literature, essays, poems, and even novels—in short, all the means by which a literate people communicates with one another, not excluding popular song. This great variety in modes of expression has already been suggested by the selections that appear in this volume.

Fortunately, a number of trustworthy guides exist for this vast literature. The classic study of Manifest Destiny is Albert K. Weinberg's *Manifest Destiny: A Study of Nationalist Expansionism in American History* (Baltimore, 1935). This has since been supplemented but not superseded by Frederick Merk, *Manifest Destiny and Mission in American History: A Reinterpretation* (New York, 1963). Weinberg describes and analyzes the whole spectrum of relevant documents; Merk emphasizes documents believed to express influential public opinion surrounding such specific events as the acquisitions of Texas, California, and Oregon—that is, press propaganda, Congressional speeches, and "orations on the hustings." Though neither volume contains a formal bibliographical appendix, one can piece together for himself a good working guide to primary sources by consulting the index and footnotes to these volumes. I know of no better place to begin.

Of the works, or documentary collections, that contain critical bibliographical essays, the best is by Norman A. Graebner in his compilation, *Manifest Destiny* (Indianapolis, Ind., 1968), pp. lxxiv–lxxxii. This bibliography is especially rich in considering the wealth of scholarship that has tilled this particular vineyard, but it also helps the advanced student in finding his way

among primary sources. A limitation reflecting its author's scholarly bias (of which more hereafter) is that it confines its attention mainly to documents bearing on the period 1835 to 1860. A
particularly fine bibliographical essay for a later period of overseas expansion that is very conscientious about the need for consulting documentary archives here and abroad is that of Richard
H. Miller in his edition of *American Imperialism in 1898:
The Quest for National Fulfillment* (New York and London,
1970), pp. 191–206. Other valuable documentary collections
with appended bibliographies include Virginia Irving Armstrong,
ed., *I Have Spoken: American History Through the Voices of
the Indians* (Chicago, 1971); Louis Filler and Allen Guttmann,
eds., *The Removal of the Cherokee Nation: Manifest Destiny or
National Dishonor?* (Boston, 1962); and Theodore P. Greene,
ed., *American Imperialism in 1898* (Boston, 1955). I know of
no bibliographical aides for the student who would pursue the
history of Manifest Destiny beyond the year 1916.

The year 1916 marked General Pershing's excursion into
Mexico (without consequence for territorial expansion) and also
the formal beginning of a global involvement not yet ended to
which the old rhetoric of Manifest Destiny seems not to apply.
Many historians, however, date this involvement from the Spanish-American War in 1898, during which Manifest Destiny was
invoked to justify overseas expansion. Among the important re-
flective essays written during this period that noted a radical departure from traditional "isolationist" policy and also a new twist
given to Manifest Destiny are H. H. Powers, "The War as a
Suggestion of Manifest Destiny," *Annals of the American Acad-
emy of Political and Social Science, XII* (September 1898),
173–192; and Carl Schurz, "Manifest Destiny," *Harper's New
Monthly Magazine, LXXXVII* (1893), 737–746, which analyzes pressures leading to the annexation of Hawaii. A more recent historian, Richard Hofstadter, has developed a theory of
"psychic crisis" related to profound economic and industrial
stress during this period to explain its expansionary pressures.
His revised essay, "Cuba, the Philippines and Manifest Destiny,"
appears in his *The Paranoid Style in American Politics and Other Essays* (New York, 1965), pp. 145–187. Julius W. Pratt,
writing on "The Ideology of Expansion" in Avery O. Craven,

ed., *Essays in Honor of William E. Dodd* (Chicago, 1935), pp. 335–353, argues a leading role in such expansion for Manifest Destiny, whose chief advocates, he finds, were not attached to economic interests. "Even those who stressed the economic value of new possessions," he writes, "could not refrain from claiming the special interest of Providence."

Professors Merk and Graebner, in the works cited above, would restrict the meaning of Manifest Destiny to continental expansion ending at the Pacific shore. They also tend to minimize its role in determining the limits of this expansion, which fell far short of its pretensions to "all Mexico" or "All North America." But H. H. Powers, in his 1898 essay, read Manifest Destiny to mean that we Americans "instinctively want the earth" as trustees of a superior civilization. Influential works promoting what I have called "The Civilization Trust" include John R. Dos Passos, *The Anglo-Saxon Century and the Unification of the English-Speaking People,* second edition (New York and London, 1903); Benjamin Kidd, *The Control of the Tropics* (New York and London, 1898); Alfred Thayer Mahan, *The Interest of America in Sea Power, Present and Future* (Boston, 1897); William Thomas Stead, *The Americanization of the World, or, The Trend of the Twentieth Century* (London and New York, 1901); and Josiah Strong, *Our Country: Its Possible Future and Its Present Crisis* (New York, 1885). These works furnish some basis for a belief that Manifest Destiny continued to figure importantly between 1900 and 1916 in the expansion of American influence, if not territorial ambition, into Central and South America. Very suggestive in this context is Samuel Crowther's proseltyzing history, *The Romance and Rise of the American Tropics* (Garden City, N. Y., 1929), which applauds the United Fruit Company for showing the way to a new kind of benevolent empire without military conquest, colonial dependency, or acquisition.

Although there can be little doubt that this southward thrust since 1900 was largely a matter of private business enterprise and "dollar diplomacy," one often hears the language of Manifest Destiny and detects the influence of Benjamin Kidd in its justification. American interest in this region from early to late is the subject of Albert Z. Carr, *The World and William Walker*

(New York, 1963); Eugene R. Huck and Edward H. Moseley, eds., *Militarists, Merchants, and Missionaries: United States Expansion in Middle America* (Tuscaloosa, Ala., 1970); Alfred Barnaby Thomas, "Puerto Rico: Our Moral Outpost," *The Delphian Quarterly,* Vol. 38, no. 1 (Winter 1955), 19–22, 35; and Edward Seccomb Wallace, *Destiny and Glory* (New York, 1957). This is to neglect an immense literature on the history of inter-American relations in the interest of a few works that help to clarify the role of Manifest Destiny in this history. A useful guide to major issues raised by this literature is Peter Nehemkis, *Latin America: Myth and Reality,* revised edition (New York and Toronto, 1966), which begins with the chapter, "The Setting for Salvation." The northward thrust to Alaska, in which Manifest Destiny is clearly the dominant consideration, is adumbrated in *The Works of William H. Seward,* 5 vols. (Boston, 1884); Morgan B. Sherwood, ed., *Alaska and its History* (Seattle and London, 1967); and Archie W. Shiels, *The Purchase of Alaska* (Alaska, 1967).

American designs on "contiguous" territories is the special subject of D. F. Warner, *The Idea of Continental Union: Agitation for the Annexation of Canada to the United States,* (Lexington, Ky., 1960); John D. P. Fuller, *The Movement for the Acquisition of All Mexico, 1846–1848* (Baltimore, Md., 1936); and Mary W. Williams, *Anglo-American Isthmian Diplomacy, 1815–1915* (Washington, D. C., 1916). The standard treatment of designs on Cuba is Philip S. Foner, *A History of Cuba and Its Relations with the United States,* 2 vols. (New York, 1963). One may judge for himself what part the Monroe Doctrine may have played in encouraging the expansion of American influence south of the border by reading Dexter Perkins' *The Monroe Doctrine, 1826–1867* (Baltimore, Md., 1933) and *The Monroe Doctrine, 1867–1907* (Baltimore, Md., 1937).

Two sharply conflicting views of Manifest Destiny's role in American expansion are Norman A. Graebner, *Empire on the Pacific: A Study in American Continental Expansion* (New York, 1955) and Richard W. Van Alstyne, *The Rising American Empire* (New York, 1960). An important recent contribution to this debate is Richard O'Connor, *Pacific Destiny: An Informal History of the U.S. in the Far East, 1776–1968* (Boston and Toronto, 1969). This work and D. F. Fleming's *America's Role in Asia* (New York, 1969) find Manifest Destiny at work even in Vietnam during the late 1960s. An additional work that, by implication at least, also contradicts the widely held view that "Imperialism was the antithesis of Manifest Destiny" is Dee Brown's *Bury My Heart at Wounded Knee: An Indian History of the American West* (New York, Chicago, and San Francisco, 1970). One should also consult, Ronald Steel, *Pax Americana* (New York, 1967), for his analysis of designs for American world supremacy.

A judicious foreign view, James Bryce's "Foreign Policy and Territorial Expansion," in his *The American Commonwealth* (New York and London, 1901), II, 531–534, stresses American restraint as it is reflected in the Monroe Doctrine and by comparison with European territorial ambition. For a recent Canadian perspective, an interesting work is Kenneth W. McNaught's short history of the United States (with John T. Saywell and John C. Ricker) entitled *Manifest Destiny*, a title that subtly organizes the whole. Its authors conclude that "in the post-[World War II] world, as in previous American history, the United States gave evidence of a sense of destiny." Other, more general works on which I have drawn include my own *The Quest for Paradise: Europe and the American Moral Imagination* (Urbana, Ill., 1961), which extends the view of American destiny in the West presented by Henry Nash Smith, *Virgin Land* (Cambridge, Mass., 1950); Edward M. Burns, *The American Idea of Mission: Concepts of National Purpose and Identity* (New Brunswick, N. J., 1957); and D. F. Fleming, *The Cold War and its Origins,* second edition, 2 vols. (Garden City, N. Y., 1968). A valuable critique of imperialist thought is A. P. Thornton, *Doctrines of Imperialism* (New York, 1965).